T0151168

"I have known Matt for many years and can vouch that he is a living example of everything written in *Work-Passion-Life Balance*. Matt has always had the propensity to take on so much more than your average Joe. He's a practicing doctor, a full-time CEO of a multi-million-dollar company with double-digit growth year after year; he's also involved with a third company with the potential to be a unicorn and on the board of the Entrepreneurs' Organization. If that's not enough, he is a super dedicated husband and father to a beautiful girl and a soon-to-be baby boy.

When you read this book, you'll understand how Matt's mind is assembled and why he doesn't burn out and continues to hit all the chords to his one-person symphony. *Work-Passion-Life Balance* is a must-read if you know you are created for something special and you want to stop saying yes to every opportunity and focus on the things that bring you joy."

—Naim Hamdar, EVP/Managing Partner, CardConnect, FL

"In *Work-Passion-Life Balance*, Matthew Kolinski sums up the best practices for a life worth living via real-life experiences and practical examples to help us all have a future to live into that is empowering."

—Chris Krimitsos, author of *Start Ugly* and founder of www.PodfestExpo.com

"Matt is one of those rare serial entrepreneurs that you hear and read about. He has an uncanny ability to juggle multiple pursuits all while bringing positive energy to everything he does."

—Nitesh Sapra, Managing Principal, Nitneil Partners

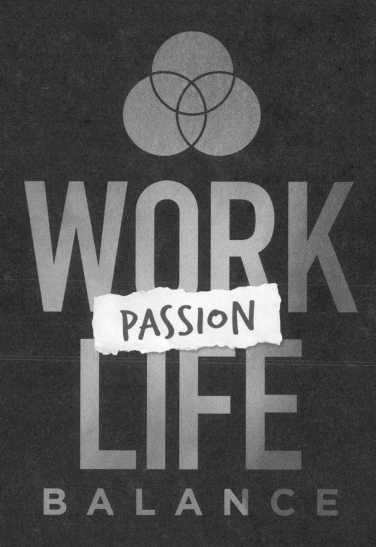

DR. MATTHEW KOLINSKI

WORK
PASSION
LIFE
BALANCE

FINDING FULFILLMENT THROUGH
ZONES OF EFFICIENCY

Advantage®

Published by Advantage, Charleston, South Carolina.
Member of Advantage Media Group.

ADVANTAGE is a registered trademark, and the Advantage colophon is a trademark of Advantage Media Group, Inc.

Printed in the United States of America.

10 9 8 7 6 5 4 3 2 1

ISBN: 978-1-64225-117-3
LCCN: 2020901730

Cover and layout design by David Taylor.

This publication is designed to provide accurate and authoritative information in regard to the subject matter covered. It is sold with the understanding that the publisher is not engaged in rendering legal, accounting, or other professional services. If legal advice or other expert assistance is required, the services of a competent professional person should be sought.

Advantage Media Group is proud to be a part of the Tree Neutral® program. Tree Neutral offsets the number of trees consumed in the production and printing of this book by taking proactive steps such as planting trees in direct proportion to the number of trees used to print books. To learn more about Tree Neutral, please visit www.treeneutral.com.

Advantage Media Group is a publisher of business, self-improvement, and professional development books and online learning. We help entrepreneurs, business leaders, and professionals share their Stories, Passion, and Knowledge to help others Learn & Grow. Do you have a manuscript or book idea that you would like us to consider for publishing? Please visit advantagefamily.com or call 1.866.775.1696.

This book is dedicated to Hannah and Nathan. May you both have a truly magnificent life ahead of you!

Acknowledgments

I would like to acknowledge my parents for providing opportunities to explore many passions and my grandma for being a role model on how to truly live a fulfilled life. I would also like to acknowledge my EO Forum for continuing to support me in all areas of my life and for constantly pushing me to be the best version possible. Most importantly, I would like to acknowledge my wonderful wife, Laura, who continues to be an amazing, supporting, and loving person and who followed me to Tampa as I explored my passion for entrepreneurship.

Contents

Beginning Your Balancing Act

*A balanced life provides the foundation
for ultimate life satisfaction.*

—*Matthew Kolinski*

"When am I going to find the time?"

How often do you ask yourself that question during a typical day? If you're like most people I know, probably more than a hundred times.

Yes, I'm exaggerating, but not by much. As a culture, we have too many emails and texts to answer. Too many things to read and watch. Too many social media notifications. And that just covers the time you spend on your phone. Then there's your *actual* life, where you have too many errands to run, too many family responsibilities to attend to, too many friends to keep in touch with, too many problems to solve at work, and way too many cars on the road

1

between where you are and where you need to go.

Actually, when you think of it, there's too much of *everything*—even TV shows. Scroll through the Netflix listings sometime, and try to count how many series they have that you've never even heard of.

Yes, life is more hectic and overstuffed than it's ever been in human history—which makes the need to achieve *balance* in your life all the more crucial.

My generation (the millennials) might not have coined the idea and term "work-life balance," but we have definitely tried to take advantage of this idea through negotiations for jobs and trying to get out of doing extra work. While this was a great start to understanding a dynamic shift in the approach to work, I believe that there is one crucial piece that is missing from this equation: passion. I live according to a philosophy I call "Work-Passion-Life Balance." This philosophy of life has been designed and created based on not only my own experiences but also the experiences of others and the ideas of great new age thinkers. I am going to show you how this philosophy takes the initial if-then statement of work-life (*if* you're working, *then* you're not living) and transforms it into a philosophy by which you have complete control of the satisfaction and fulfillment you have every day of your life. Work-Passion-Life Balance is going to be the new answer to the interview questions, personal statements, and blog posts that everyone from all ages will be using because it provides a new level of understanding about both *how* to be satisfied and *how much* fulfillment you can have in your everyday living.

What do I mean by balance? It's this: you're able to structure your life in such a way that you can attend to all the important areas in your life and find personal satisfaction. It's using "Zones of Efficiency" (more on them later) to maximize your overlap between Work-Passion-Life in such a way that you feel satisfied with the three main areas of your life and most importantly so that you create a way to keep it balanced. You've hit what Robert De Niro's character calls in the Martin Scorsese movie *New York, New York*, a major chord—you have people you love in your life, you're making enough money to be comfortable, and you're doing something you find fulfilling. Sure, you still have periods of time when everything seems overwhelming for one reason or another; that's just how life goes sometimes. However, when it comes to the big picture, you're taking care not to neglect anything that's vital to your happiness or the happiness of the most important people in your life.

Hitting this major chord can make for sweet music indeed, but they can be tricky notes to reach. It's worth the effort however. And once you figure out how to stay on key, everyone will be singing your praises. Without balance, you'll find yourself hitting way too many sour notes.

Recently, I checked out synonyms for the word *unbalanced*—and the list I ended up with is definitely not pretty. Here are a few alternatives: *deranged, demented, crazed, troubled, disturbed, unhinged, insane, mad, mad as a hatter, mad as a March hare, raving mad, out of one's mind, not in one's right mind, neurotic, psychotic, crazy, loopy, loony, mixed up, nuts, nutty, nutty as a fruitcake, bananas, cracked, crackpot, daft, dippy, screwy, with a screw loose, batty, dotty, cuckoo, bonkers, potty, mental, screwed up, not all there, off one's head, out of one's head, out to lunch, a bit lacking, round the bend, round the twist, crackers, barking, barking mad, off one's rocker, nutso, squirrelly, wacko,* and *buggy.*

And I even left some out. Yes. It's clear, at least to *Roget's Thesaurus*, that being unbalanced is definitely not good for your mental health.

Now, I don't mean to imply everyone who is living an out-of-balance life is completely insane. However, I learned for myself from the times when my life was completely out of whack that I wasn't exactly seeing things very clearly. Being out of balance *does* affect the way you think and behave. It affects your emotions and your relationships, usually in a negative way. When you direct all your energies at one part of your life at the expense of all the others, something has to give.

And you don't want that something to be *you*.

***

My name is Matthew Kolinski, and I am a thirty-five-year-old physician, entrepreneur, husband, father, son, brother, friend, cousin, nephew, business partner, consultant, mentor, author, and business owner who has had difficulty keeping his life in balance. I was born and raised in a south suburb of Chicago, but I now live in sunny Tampa, Florida, where I have the ability to live out my Work-Passion-Life Balanced lifestyle every day!

I have had multiple failures in my life, but through my failures I believe I have found a method to the madness of balancing all the different roles that define me. More importantly, I believe this model can be used by anyone who would like a guide to finding ultimate life satisfaction by acknowledging the three main areas that define every one of us and finding ways to efficiently put them into perspective. As you can see, I have a lot on my plate, and if I hadn't learned how to achieve balance by now, well, most of my friends would probably use one of Roget's unpleasant words to describe my state of mind—or to put it another way, as Matthew McConaughey's character in *Wolf of Wall Street* said, I would have "split my differential and [tipped] the f*** over, or worse yet, [imploded]."

Was it easy to find balance? Not at all. I've had to learn some tough lessons along the way. The education I gained from all my experiences, however, has been priceless. It's taught me the importance of covering all the bases when it comes to living a well-rounded life.

4

Most of all, it's taught me the importance of identifying and acknowledging my *passions* and putting them into perspective when it comes to the way they impact my work and my life.

When most people talk about balance, they're usually just referring to the two big-ticket items everyone has to juggle—work or life. In other words, it is often used as an excuse for millennials to work from home or have unlimited paid time off, as seen at large tech firms. The problem with this thought process is it is an "or" statement, similar to a seesaw. You are either working or you are living. In my own life, I discovered just addressing those two meant one crucial ingredient went missing from the mix, and that ingredient was *passion*. So with this book, I'm out to rid society of the phrase "work-life balance" and replace this incomplete picture with my own philosophy of achieving Work-Passion-Life Balance. I might be a little too late to help my fellow millennials pursue the accommodation of this new trio from their employers, but, after this, hopefully future generations will know what to ask for, and more importantly, people of all ages will use this philosophy to evaluate their own lives and potentially make small changes to their approaches to everyday decisions.

Here's why I believe passion must be added to any consideration of how you're focusing your time and energy: No matter what you're doing in life, if passion isn't an important component of it, your waking hours can quickly seem like drudgery. To me, it's essential to wake up with something to look forward to, something that excites and inspires you, something

> **No matter what you're doing in life, if passion isn't an important component of it, your waking hours can quickly seem like drudgery.**

that makes you want to get out of bed and take on the world. Passion is almost like a calling—it's a hunger to connect with something outside of yourself. It makes you feel like you'll never feel satisfied unless you make that connection in a profound way.

Your inner compass will often lead you to your passions and sometimes at a very young age. For example, when I was in kindergarten, the teacher asked us all to draw what we wanted to be when we grew up. I didn't hesitate. I drew myself as a doctor. It's what I felt as a kid. It was my *passion*. And that passion never left me. As a matter of fact, as I progressed through grammar school and high school, that goal became more and more important to me. There were three reasons that ultimately shaped this desire from a young age that have had a huge impact on my entire life.

First reason? I was positively impacted by my own pediatrician, Dr. Germino, and I saw that he was his own boss with his name on the door! I wanted to be my own boss. My dad worked extremely hard for a big company—and even though he did his job well enough to rise through the ranks over the years, his job security was rarely a sure thing. I personally felt that uncertainty when his employers went through various mergers and acquisitions and he was in danger of being downsized, even though, thankfully, that fear was only realized during one of these events. Still, it was a fear and a profound one. I believed at an early age that becoming a physician would keep that fear from being an active part of my emotional life and that I could control my destiny in a positive way.

The second reason? Financial stability. I grew up on the South Side of Chicago in a tight-knit middle-class family. I wouldn't trade that experience for the world, but I wanted something better for myself as an adult. As the oldest of three kids (I have a younger brother and sister), it was difficult watching my parents scramble to pay for our Catholic school tuition and supplies, our involvement in sports teams, and the modest family vacations we managed to take. It left me wanting to ensure my financial stability as an adult and grow beyond my middle-class roots. Money was still very tight during my childhood despite my mom also working various jobs, such as teaching preschool. Our difficult financial circumstances put a tremendous burden on my parents, and that made me resolve to never leave my professional fate in other people's hands.

Finally, I wanted to be able to give back and have an impact on my community. Dr. Germino had a profound impact on me here as well. If I was successful in my chosen profession in medicine, it would provide me with the time and means to have an impact on whatever community I ended up joining. My grandma was a role model in this area as well because she was a generous person who gave of her time, energy, and self whenever possible to her church, community, and family. I saw myself contributing in a myriad of ways—by employing others, by serving as a positive influence on others, and by donating money to help others who had their own financial struggles.

But a funny thing happened along the way to becoming a doctor. I realized that, deep down, I was also an entrepreneur. And I realized that being an entrepreneur also accomplished those same three motivations I just shared. I was determined to combine my two professional passions, which created the unique pathway I ultimately chose. (I'll explain more shortly.) Interestingly, in the late 1980s and early '90s, most physicians were entrepreneurs who ran their own practices, so the overlap, at the time, was unknowingly a perfect match. Unfortunately, that changed during the twelve years I went through college and medical training, which left me in a challenging situation (another thing I'll discuss later).

How did I find my way to entrepreneurship? Well, at a young

age, due to the family financial strains I already described, I typically had two to three summer jobs or after-school jobs. This started as early as seventh grade. I had my eye out for ways to bring in more money for my family and myself. That began with doing odd jobs for neighbors and relatives (one of the great things about my childhood was my grandparents lived just a couple of streets away) and culminated with my first "official" business in high school, "Handy Matt's."

While my one-man firm never quite made it to multinational corporation status, it did provide a few profitable summers. When I was considering what kind of business I should try, I wanted to zero in on a task that pretty much every homeowner hated to do because that meant they would be willing to pay someone else to do it. Well, *nobody* enjoyed painting—especially when it came to giving the ceiling a fresh coat. So I mastered that art and thus Handy Matt's was born. My first client? Grandma.

Wanting to make the operation as professional as possible, I invoiced for my time and kept all my receipts for materials so I could submit "expense reports" to my customers for reimbursement. For some reason, doing real business paperwork was exciting to me. Okay, maybe I was a weird teenager. The more likely explanation was it made me feel as though I were a real businessman without the constraints of having a boss.

At the time, I didn't think of running my own business as a passion. It was just a way to make money without having to work for anybody else. The fact that I loved it was just a side benefit. That's why, when I attended college at Loyola University Chicago in 2002, I looked for more opportunities in that direction. During my junior year, I found one. I joined up with a few of my fellow classmates to write résumés for graduating students who were looking for permanent work—and we did this for the low, low price of ninety-nine dollars apiece. Yes, we, the lowly underclassmen, were helping seniors start their careers!

However, I was also helping *myself* start a new career in an entrepreneurial space in which I still operate to this day: staffing and recruiting. The economy was pretty rocky when I was in college (2002–2006)—the tech bubble had just popped, and the world was on its way to the Great Recession, so college kids were naturally having trouble finding positions. Less people were retiring, and companies were afraid to expand their internal staffs due to budgetary uncertainties. I immediately thought there was a business in that, and it sure beat painting ceilings.

So some of us in the résumé-writing business decided to start a company called Superior Business Staffing to help connect potential employers with qualified graduates who needed work. We found the best way to ease these grads into permanent positions was to obtain contracts with customers for temporary positions so they could first prove themselves to the company. This also allowed the hiring managers to justify the increase in their budget for internal employees.

But that in turn gave us a new challenge. Temporary workers are traditionally paid and insured by the temp agency that supplies them, not the end customer. That meant we needed to handle time cards, weekly payroll, and payroll taxes in addition to covering our candidates with workers' compensation insurance and general liability insurance. As you may remember from my experience with Handy Matt's, I'm one of the few people in the world who loves to dive into paperwork—so even though we were running this business during the nights and weekends on a shoestring, we somehow managed to secure a loan for overhead including the insurance, and we found a payroll funding company willing to work with us to provide weekly paychecks to our employees. It was pretty amazing to realize we could actually pull all that off.

***

After I graduated from Loyola, I went on to a very expensive and stressful medical school education through which I racked up over $250,000 in initial student loan debt that ultimately incurred interest for almost ten years before I was able to start making significant payments. (Thank you, government loans, for adding interest while I was already in school and then making only minimum wage in residency.) The loans nearly doubled due to the 8 percent interest rate over the ten years. As a result, when I finally completed residency and was able to start repaying my loans, the grand total had skyrocketed to over $400,000.

I couldn't help having money (or the lack of it) on my mind once again. So during my last year of medical school, I shut down Superior Business Staffing and used my same vendors to start up the Authorized Dealer program under the banner of a new company, USA Staffing Services. I still focused on providing the back-office operational support structures for temporary workers, but instead of having an internal sales team, we used existing recruitment companies that had their own connections, and they performed their own recruiting and customer acquisition. Our Authorized Dealer program was unique and in some ways modeled a car dealership. Sure, all Ford vehicles are created equally, but people buy them from their local Ford dealership due to personal relationships and convenient location; in the same manner, our temporary workers were being sold by local recruitment firms that were great at sales. This was our way of flipping the staffing industry upside down and empowering entrepreneurs to provide full-service recruiting and staffing to their existing customers. And thanks to the rapidly growing internet of the time, we were able to offer our services to recruitment companies all across the country.

I started my medical residency three months after I started my new company in 2010. I was accepted into a very rigorous four-year program instead of the usual three because I was doing combined adult and pediatric medical training. If you know anything about residency, you know the hours are brutal—an average of anywhere between seventy to eighty hours every week. At the same time, I was putting countless hours into the start-up of my new business to make USA Staffing Services so successful, it would eventually pay off my student debt for me. Then I could be the full-time doctor I wanted to be without that financial pressure hanging over my head for who knows how many years.

But as John Lennon once said, "Life is what happens to you when you're busy making other plans." Well, life definitely happened to me in October of 2013, when I was finishing up my residency and I ran into a major issue with the business.

One of the lynchpins of my staffing business was our ability to insure our temps with workers' comp insurance. So it was a pretty good kick in the stomach when, out of nowhere, I received a notice saying my current policy was being canceled for no good reason. At the time, we were billing a million dollars in revenue a year, but we were barely profitable due to our overhead. I could have easily gotten another policy, but I was worn out and wanted some outside help to take the business to the next level.

Luckily, for the past year, I had been talking with another entrepreneur, Mark Curtiss, about partnering with me on USA Staffing. He ran a similar business, and it seemed like teaming up might be good for both of us. The workers' comp crisis brought those discussions to a head. Mark had the financing, the logistics, and a whole team in place to hopefully take the company to the next level. Since I was planning to primarily be a doctor at that time, it was a good moment to take a back seat in the business I had started. So I brought him in as majority owner, retaining 49 percent of the company shares.

Even though the company had been my baby, letting it go felt like the right move for me at that time. I was about to start that demanding fellowship, which was in Milwaukee, and that had to be my top priority based on social norms and the fact that I was accepted into a strong fellowship program. By keeping a substantial investment in my old company, however, I could make a good-sized residual income to pay off those med school loans. It felt like a foolproof plan. Once I worked out all the kinks of the agreement with Mark (who is still my partner to this day, by the way), I finished up the last six months of my residency and began my fellowship in July of the next year. And that's when it hit me.

The fellowship wasn't doing it for me. I wasn't feeling it. I thoroughly enjoyed my patient interactions, and I felt deep connections with those I served, but it didn't bring me the life satisfaction I had hoped for. I had just completed four years of brutal medical education followed by four years of residency training, and now I was looking at another few years of being treated as an employee and student in the fellowship program. The difference was that I was now a full-fledged, licensed doctor. And I loved being a doctor. I loved taking care of patients. The passion was there for that kind of medical work, and it still is today. The problem was the fellowship itself. Chalk it up to my entrepreneurial spirit, but I was at a point in my life where I wanted to *be* a doctor, not continue to be a trainee in a new specialty.

More importantly, I realized for the first time that running my own businesses hadn't just been about money. It was one of my *passions*—a passion I desperately missed. I felt like I had lost my baby, and I needed it back.

And my baby needed me as well.

USA Staffing wasn't growing like I had expected it to when I stepped away, so I began to involve myself more with its management. I don't blame Mark; he already had his own business to run, and he just didn't have the time to put into the one I had handed over to him. Things were moving too slowly for my liking. So only a few months into the fellowship, I pulled the plug. I told the powers that be I would go ahead and finish the first year, which ended in June of 2015. After that, however, I was done.

I would also have to move. When Mark took over the company, he took its operation to the city where he lived: Tampa, Florida. I still remember the call I had with Mark when I talked with him about rejoining the team on a full-time basis, and we both were excited about this next phase. On July 1, 2015, that's where I, along with my girlfriend Laura (now my wife) and Millie, our beloved goldendoodle, ended up too. I made arrangements to work night shifts for one week out of the month at a hospital back in Milwaukee. The other three weeks? Well, I would finally be a full-time entrepreneur for the first time since I ran Handy Matt's. And that gave me an awesome feeling.

Finally, I felt like I had achieved the perfect Work-Passion-Life Balance. I could do the medical work I loved to do and still have a big chunk of the month available to devote 100 percent of my time to growing my business. I could satisfy the multiple passions in my life and still have the time to start a family. (I proposed to Laura in December of 2015, and we were married the following October.) It's a lifestyle I still enjoy to this day. Plus, I have to say, Florida winters are a lot easier to take than the ones in Chicago or Milwaukee.

In my mind, I've finally hit that major chord I wrote about

earlier in this intro, all because I learned a truth I will never forget for the rest of my life.

> **In order to have a truly fulfilling life, you must always find a way for your work, your passion, and your personal life to live in balance.**

In order to have a truly fulfilling life, you must always find a way for your work, your passion, and your personal life to live in balance. That's the only way you can have true satisfaction and fulfillment. More importantly, the way in which you balance these three key areas of life is what I want to share with as many people as possible. This philosophy has the magic that is missing from most people, and I look forward to sharing it in detail so everyone can find fulfillment in their life.

As a result of achieving that balance, I've prospered both financially and emotionally. As I write these words, USA Staffing is about to celebrate its tenth anniversary. I have a contract with a hospital to serve as a doctor there for one week out of every month. And I'm proud to say Laura and I now have a beautiful sixteen-month-old daughter, Hannah, with child number two on the way!

***

Now what about you? How's your balancing act going?

If you've been finding yourself tilting a little too far one way or the other, I'm hoping I can help you straighten out and fly right by sharing my own experiences and whatever wisdom I've gained from them. You undoubtedly have different passions and priorities than me. And that's fine. But I believe what I've learned is universal and can be applied to anyone's life.

Yes, I know many great minds have already offered a lot of awesome advice in the past about how best to find balance between work and life. However, as I stated earlier, I intend to go beyond the traditional work-life model you'll find elsewhere because I believe that model is too limiting for reasons you'll discover in this book.

The bottom line is this: when you acknowledge the third component of passion as an essential ingredient in your balanced life, you create a whole new level of joy, satisfaction, and fulfillment in your life. You experience a level of pride, accomplishment, and excitement that you otherwise would miss out on.

Ready to hit your own personal major chord in life? Then read on, and find out what I have to share in the pages to come, and maybe you'll end up as blessed as I am.

The Circles of Life

*You will never find time for anything. If
you want time you must make it.*

—Charles Buxton

In *The Lion King*, they famously sing about the circle of life. Well, the truth is I believe there are *three* "circles of life": work, passion, and life, as I discussed in the introduction. All three circles can be viewed through the lens of the relationships and energy associated with the various areas of your life. Here's how I define them.

Work is traditionally thought of as what you do to earn a living. In this book I consider this the selfless circle of your day-to-day hours. This category covers those relationships that are primarily selfless and for the benefit of another person (usually in terms of an employee-employer relationship). At its core, work is a necessary part of living and is usually viewed in a negative way. Spoiler alert: it doesn't have to be. Work can also be the relationships that are one sided outside of your job. In all cases, this area predominately involves selfless energy.

> **At its core, work is a necessary part of living and is usually viewed in a negative way. Spoiler alert: it doesn't have to be.**

Life is composed mostly of your personal relationships that are **mutually beneficial**. These relationships should be give and take and not one sided. Your family members and your friends all fall into this circle, but other relationships from the other two circles can fall into here as well. More on that later.

Finally, *passion* is an intangible that lights the fire in your belly and makes you excited about getting up in the morning. This circle is typically a **selfish** relationship with yourself, as you don't necessarily need anyone else to be a part of this activity for you to find enjoyment in it. Passion is something you feel deep inside—it almost feels like a calling, and it is the task or activity you would do if you were rich enough not to need to be employed. But it may have the potential to make you some cash. I'll talk about that near the end of the book.

When the circles overlap with each other, as demonstrated above, they form three areas of satisfaction that I call "Zones of Efficiency." I will speak about each one of these Zones of Efficiency individually throughout this book. In the very center is the area where all three core attributes overlap, and to me this center section represents the amount of balance and life fulfillment one has. I call the center the "Zone of Life Satisfaction." As you will see, the larger the overlap of the three core attributes, the larger your fulfillment with all things related to personal satisfaction.

Throughout the pages to come, I'll be exploring each of these three concepts in depth. I'll offer the lessons my own experience has taught me about them and how I've been able to attain a balance that accommodates each one of them.

Attaining life satisfaction using the Work-Passion-Life Balance model is difficult at times because it's never a static model. There are times when, out of necessity, one of the three circles ends up dominating my day. The birth of my daughter, Hannah, a year and a half ago, for example, couldn't help but shift some priorities toward the life space (not that I'm complaining!). Similarly, when I'm on my night shifts at the hospital and performing my doctor duties, my medical work naturally must take precedence, so I focus on patient relationships more than my family relationships.

However, balance to me isn't about achieving a perfect symmetry every single day. Sometimes it's about devoting a day to strictly family activities, and sometimes it's about pulling an all-nighter at work when I'm trying to get a project off the ground. Life demands a dynamic approach, so I try to stay flexible and open to what's happening at the moment. At the same time, I also make the effort to schedule time for everything that's important to me. When you have strong relationships and acknowledge the three components, then your support network should also understand why you must work those extra hours at the office or spend time on your personal project to maintain your balance.

> **Life demands a dynamic approach, so I try to stay flexible and open to what's happening at the moment.**

That wasn't always the case. I've already shared one example of a time when my life was extremely out of balance, and I will be sharing a few more as we move along. I'm not perfect—if you don't believe me, ask my wife. My hope, however, is you're able to learn from my past mistakes and, in so doing, avoid making them yourself.

More than that, I hope you can gain some insight from my ups and downs and apply the insight I've gained from them to your own life. While it's true that experience is the best teacher, it doesn't have to be *your* experience you learn from. I've soaked up many a crucial lesson just from observing others, which is why I think my personal journey may be of benefit to you. In the pages to come, I will reveal what the circles of work, life, and passion mean to me and how I weave them together in my day-to-day life. As I do so, I invite you to reflect on your own personal attitude toward each, as well as evaluate how well you're integrating the circles into your own life.

I have divided this book into four sections: section 1, "Work + Passion + Life," is made up of chapters 1, 2, and 3, and these introduce the concepts and the separate components needed to establish an understanding of why they are important. Section 2, "The Zones of Efficiency," includes chapters 4, 5, 6, and 7, in which I discuss how the overlap between the core attributes helps to align and reinforce your desire for alignment. In section 3, "The Zone of Life Satisfaction," I discuss how each Zone of Efficiency can converge to form a balanced and satisfied life. I end with section 4, "Entrepreneurship as a Passion," chapters 9 and 10, where I put everything together and explore how I achieved balance through entrepreneurship.

Now let's get to work … starting with work!

Work + Life + Passion

Without ambition one starts nothing.
Without work one finishes nothing. The prize
will not be sent to you. You have to win it.

—*Ralph Waldo Emerson*

CHAPTER 1

Work Is a Four-Letter Word

"Nearly every person I worked with, I saw cry at their desk."

I'm proud to say the above quote isn't from anyone who works for me. No, those are the words of one Amazon white-collar worker reflecting on his experience at the mammoth corporation.[1] CEO Jeff Bezos probably wouldn't argue with this assessment because the Amazon head believes working for him should be a bit punishing. "You can work long, hard or smart, but at Amazon.com, you can't choose two out of three," he wrote in a 1997 letter to shareholders, adding, "It's not easy to work here."

When you hear stories like that, it's understandable why many regard *work* as a dirty word and the archenemy of true balance. To them, work is something like a hamster running on a wheel, perpetu-

---

1   Jodi Kantor and David Streitfeld, "Inside Amazon: Wrestling Big Ideas in a Bruising Workplace," *New York Times,* August 15, 2015, https://www.nytimes.com/2015/08/16/technology/inside-amazon-wrestling-big-ideas-in-a-bruising-workplace.html?_r=1.

ally spinning you around in place but ultimately taking you nowhere.

And the truth is work gets a bad rap in the public eye. There are countless movies and TV shows where workaholic parents are portrayed as cold and clueless drones who ignore the needs of their loved ones on a daily basis. Usually, they have to learn a big lesson late in the story about how work isn't all *that* important. They then demonstrate their newfound interest in their family by making some big, dramatic choice—like skipping their big sales presentation to go to their child's recital or passing up a huge and demanding promotion because they're already too busy to spend time with their spouse and kids.

Most of these are, of course, false choices scripted by a screen-writer who chooses drama over reality. The truth, however, is never as simple as Hollywood would have it—and the choices are almost never that binary. In other words, you don't have to blow a big opportunity in order to be a good parent or spouse. You don't have to set a ceiling on a booming business in order to maintain important relationships. You can fulfill both roles if you manage your life correctly or, to put it a different way, if you ultimately manage the energy applied to life correctly.

Once you realize that truth, there's no reason to demonize the idea of work. Actually, it's time we gave it a little respect. Anthropologists will tell you work is a vital component of what separates us from animals. Our ability to create divisions of labor enabled us from the very beginning to tackle large tasks as a group and take care of each other more effectively than other species, which empowered us to dominate them.

Part of that ability to create divisions of labor resulted in us becoming the first known specialists. Early on, humans were able to detect who was the most proficient at a certain task and give them full rein of whatever they excelled at. True, these early experts could only specialize in primitive skills such as hunting and foraging, but this created a template we still use today. When you need something done that you can't do yourself, you go out (or more frequently these days, use an app) to find somebody who *can* do it—and do it well.

Yes, work is an intrinsic part of who we are and have been, from the beginning of our time on Earth right up until the twenty-first century. Something about the human spirit insists we should be productive and apply ourselves to creating progress for ourselves and society at large. But that doesn't mean we have to work ourselves to death—or even end up regularly

> **Work is also the time spent on relationships because even the strongest relationships in life require selfless acts at times.**

sobbing at our desks like that poor guy at Amazon. Again, *it doesn't have to be a binary choice*.

Work is also the time spent on relationships because even the strongest relationships in life require selfless acts at times. While it is true that "life relationships" should be mutually beneficial, there are always crossroads in those relationships when we have to carry out selfless acts and devote quality time to enrich our connection to another person either because of conflicts that arise or due to neglect.

But again, the time to do this kind of "work" can be arranged and folded into your schedule. It's not a binary choice. I'll admit I used to think it was. I thought everything else should take a back seat to work. And that's what deep-sixed my first marriage.

It happened when I was doing my medical residency—my life became completely *un*balanced. Some of that was a natural consequence of the enormous number of hours the residency demanded from me. The part I take responsibility for, however, was this: whatever time and energy I had left over after those seventy or so hours a week at the hospital I put into my new business—along with most of my money. I averaged only about ten bucks an hour in the residency program, then I took those earnings and reinvested them into getting USA Staffing Services off the ground. If you've ever seen that illustration of a snake eating its own tail, that's a pretty good representation of what I was going through at the time. Yet some part of me knew this investment in myself was important. However, it was a very selfish act that isolated my first wife both emotionally and mentally.

The truth was I was investing the minimum amount in my newlywed status. If you'd like to know the formula for destroying a new marriage, here it is: *spend absolutely no time* with the person you just exchanged vows with, become too emotionally spent to invest in the relationship, and allow an outside passion to devour any residual time you may have remaining at the end of the day. I made no commitment to our relationship—and that lack of commitment was a bit mutual. As a fellow physician, she had her own passion for patient care that she routinely chose over our relationship, so it was ultimately doomed from the beginning from both sides.

The unhappy result was we ended up divorced. We were both pretty young, and it may have never been a great match to begin with, but I have to take my share of the blame. My decision to focus on work actually caused damage to several relationships in my life, including those with friends, family, and work colleagues. As a result, I felt increasingly isolated. It was a very selfish period in my life that resulted in a disproportionately small area of balance.

In recent years, however, I've found I can make work work in my favor—but first, I had to reexamine my own attitudes about it.

Here's what I learned through that process.

OLD-SCHOOL WORK

Before I reveal how my attitude toward work has evolved, I'd like to take a minute and talk about what it's traditionally meant to people in the past.

First and foremost, work has usually been viewed as a dividing point between a person and their personal pursuits. There was work, and there was life, and never the twain did meet. Frankly, there was little opportunity for any overlap back then. Most people worked for large companies, either in white-collar or blue-collar jobs, and they were often just treated as cogs in a machine. The result? They considered their work hours tedious, dull, repetitive, and exhausting. But to them, there was no other choice. They *had* to work to make money. That necessity was a big part of what gave work an unsavory connotation—it couldn't possibly be enjoyable because it was only about getting paid, and you had to get paid in order to afford food, shelter, clothes, and so on.

Traditional model of work-life balance: Step one, divide the twenty-four-hour day into eight-hour segments. Step two, out of the sixteen hours of "awake time," devote eight hours to work and eight hours to personal life. Thus, the forty-hour work week was born!

When seen strictly through that very limited lens, the idea of work becomes an oppressive obligation that will weigh you down throughout your adult life. Think about a common phrase all of us have used at one time or another: "I have to go to work." *Have to.* You can't buy the necessities in life without money, so … *you have to go to work.* Like you have to go to the dentist when your gums are bleeding or you have to go to the store because you ran out of milk. You don't want to. You *have* to.

> **After all, if work is not supposed to be fun, then it has to be unpleasant. Has to be.**

Another common expression you may have heard is "It's not supposed to be fun. That's why they call it work." It's something bosses love to say when an employee complains about a particular task. Unfortunately, this is just another reinforcement of the viewpoint that in no way is work ever supposed to be enjoyable. After all, if work is *not* supposed to be fun, then it has to be unpleasant. *Has* to be. Again, another binary choice: work or fun. The two concepts can't possibly coexist, right?

No, wrong. *Really* wrong. To me, the last time people were this wrong about something is when they thought the world was flat. (I understand there are a few of those still out there, and they refuse to book a Carnival Cruise for just that reason.)

I admit, however, I bought into this bad attitude about work. When I first began starting up businesses, I assumed I was only doing it to make money. When I stayed up all night after a long medical residency shift to work on building my staffing business, I told myself I was only doing it so I could eventually pay off my student loans. I didn't even *allow* myself to think otherwise because I had been taught that work was not about pleasure in any way, shape, or form.

It wasn't until I let go of my entrepreneurial pursuits that I realized how much I missed that kind of work. Miss work? How could I miss something I thought I was doing out of necessity? If it was just about money, why did I feel a void in my life, a void that wasn't filled until I jumped back into running my own business? I didn't really give those questions much thought. After I did return to managing USA Staffing Services, however, and after I found myself spending hours there that weren't necessary just because I loved the sheer excitement of figuring out ways to grow the business, I finally came to the conclusion that running my own operation was actually ... well, fun. It felt more like a selfish passion than selfless working (more on this later).

I'm sure I'm not alone. I'm sure the overwhelming majority of people enter the job arena as I did: thinking of work as an unenjoyable chore you do in order to earn money.

The work attribute is not limited to simply the time spent earning money. It also comes into play whenever you have to make self-sacrificing decisions to spend time, money, or energy in a way that you may not necessarily choose on your own. Here are several examples of other items to add to the work bucket: struggling to connect with difficult family members, parenting (e.g., changing diapers, caring for sick kids, and dealing with difficult kids), volunteering (e.g., at soup kitchens, through a helpline, by doing church/temple work, or by running charity organizations), or even house work (e.g., yard work, cleaning, shopping, and home improvements). You may feel that several of these items are more passion focused, and you may be right; however, they are considered part of the work you do, and even though they will overlap with passion, the time and energy spent should be counted as work. The underlying passion would be considered "giving back" or "donating time," and we will see later that the overlap can create a Zone of Efficiency that will enhance your life.

CHAPTER 2

The Phenomenon of Passion in the Workplace

There is no passion to be found playing small—in settling for a life that is less than the one you are capable of living.

—Nelson Mandela

"You work too much."

"Why do you keep being an entrepreneur? Isn't it just a whole bunch of stress you don't need?"

"Stop working nights and weekends. How can you enjoy life?"

These are all actual things that have been said to me over the years. People think I'm suffering because of my work habits. My response is always the same: "I love what I'm doing. I don't consider it work."

In this chapter, I'll explore this third component of Work-Passion-Life Balance in more detail because I'm sure many of you reading this book either haven't uncovered your passion or aren't sure how to connect more strongly to the one you have. I've already related how long it took me to figure out my primary passion of entrepreneurship—and now that I have, I'd like to help guide you toward yours.

But first, let me repeat my definition of a passion—it's simply something you love to spend time doing. It may or may not involve your family and friends. It may or may not make you money. It may or may not bring you any recognition. None of this matters because you don't do it for those kinds of reasons. You do it because it's just too much fun to even think about *not* doing it. And yes, that makes it a selfish pursuit, but ultimate personal fulfillment requires some selfishness. Passion is a primary way of finding that fulfillment.

And again, your passion doesn't have to be directly connected to how you make a living. Since this is how I first started as an entrepreneur, let's use a handyman as an example—we'll call him Handyman Joe. And let's say during the day, Handyman Joe is a Mr. Fix It for the neighborhood. During the evening, however, he loves nothing more than to work in his garage building furniture, even though it's very close to what he's been doing all day—after all, he's still working with tools and doing manual labor. However, it's in a totally different and more fulfilling way. Instead of doing what other people hire him to do, he gets to do what *he* wants to do. And he also loves the feeling of making something beautiful and well constructed from scratch.

Similarly, a schoolteacher could love to paint (and I mean actual art, not ceilings like me in high school), and a grocery store clerk could totally be into golf or tennis in their spare time. A person with an office job might love writing spy novels at night for the sheer thrill of imagining themselves at the center of a pulse-pounding story.

There are literally millions of different personal passions and millions of different motivations for why people have them.

As I noted, you don't engage in these kinds of passions for the recognition (although that can be nice). You don't do it for money (although that, too, can be very nice). And you certainly don't follow these pursuits because someone talks you into them—after all, if you don't enjoy them, you'll talk yourself right back out of them. No, these kinds of passions are internally motivated and self-sustaining; they're all about what stokes the fire in your belly. You just want to do them for the sake of doing them, and you want to keep getting better and better at them.

Don't get me wrong. Even though your passion may fall outside of what you do for a day job, you can still derive a lot of pleasure from what you do for a paycheck. You can still be extremely skilled at your work and want to excel at it. What your passion adds to the mixture outside of your forty-hour week, however, is more overall life satisfaction, which in turn brings you many remarkable benefits. A study done by the Society of Behavioral Science[2] demonstrated that when you engage in pursuits you're passionate about in your leisure time, the following very awesome things happen for you:

- Your mood is overall more positive.

- You feel more life satisfaction.

- You're less prone to depression and stress.

- You experience better cardiovascular health.

You don't have to be a doctor to know that's all good stuff.

---

2   Matthew J. Zawadzki, Joshua M. Smyth, and Heather J. Costigan, "Real-Time Associations between Engaging in Leisure and Daily Health and Well-Being," February 28, 2015, https://www.ucmerced.edu/sites/ucmerced.edu/files/documents/zawadzki-paper-2015.pdf.

Before I developed the Work-Passion-Life Balance model, it was difficult to explain the concept. Now I tell people who ask how amazing it feels to have passion motivating me in my work. How it raises my mental game. How it's not stressful for me at all. And most importantly, how it's actually enjoyable—because I love doing it. Still, they have a hard time understanding how I have the energy to run my business *and* practice medicine, especially when they discover how little I sleep. I have a standard answer for that too: "I'll have time to sleep when I'm dead." Morbid and not totally accurate, but I like saying it for the shock value.

I have so much enthusiasm for my work that my internal battery never seems to run down. I don't have trouble managing my energy, only my time. I know not everyone's like me (they remind me of that fact on a regular basis), but, to me, if you love what you do every single day, every single minute of every day, and every single second of every minute of every day, then you'll have energy and drive to spare.

Frequently, the people questioning me tell me they don't feel that way. They seem to be dissatisfied with their jobs or even their entire lives. They feel like they have no time or outlet for their passions. They might tell me they love to garden, but … they don't. They might tell me they love to read, but … then admit they've only read one book in the past six months. They simply don't acknowledge the importance of their passion, whether it's fishing, hiking, arts and crafts, writing, drawing. You can literally name any activity, and it will be something someone somewhere considers their passion. Most people, when I ask them how often they get to do what they love, will say maybe one week out of the year, when they take a vacation. And I'm shocked.

So what about the other fifty-one weeks? They do without their passion, as well as the energy and drive that passion provides.

They can't figure me out because they haven't figured out how to get that kind of fulfillment in their lives on a regular basis. They actually seem more stressed than me, even though I put in a whole lot more hours than they do, because their work just makes them feel tired as opposed to excited. I understand that feeling because I've experienced it myself. If passion is minimized, that typically means the other two categories, work and life, are taking up too much space. In my formula, it's not mandatory to earn income performing your passion, but it is extremely important to acknowledge your passion and make room for it in your life on a regular basis.

> **In my formula, it's not mandatory to earn income performing your passion, but it is extremely important to acknowledge your passion and make room for it in your life on a regular basis.**

Many people may disagree with me, but if you ignore what you love to do, then how can you have ultimate life satisfaction?

WHAT'S MISSING FROM THIS PICTURE?

It took me all of three months to realize I had lost something vital in my life.

I'm talking about the time when I was still in my medical residency, when I decided to let go of my USA Staffing business and focus on my future as a doctor. As I talked about in the introduction to this book, I made that call in October of 2013, and it felt like somebody had taken a huge weight off my chest … initially. For the first time in years, I didn't have the financial pressure of paying our temps, our own employees, and the overhead for the business. The truth was that after years of working insane hospital hours combined with endless efforts to get USA off the ground, I was exhausted. Looking back, it was probably more the four years of eighty-hour work weeks than any specific activity I was engaged in that had burnt me out. But at the time, all I knew was I had to let go of something. And since I was about to enter into a demanding medical fellowship, that something had to be my entrepreneurial efforts, or so I thought.

My relief lasted through the holiday season—Christmas can be a great distraction from regular life. But then, in early January, something began to gnaw at me, a vague sense of dissatisfaction. More alarmingly, I felt like I wasn't thinking at the same level. I was used to constantly thinking creatively when I was tackling business problems, and that mindset spilled over into creative problem-solving in my residency work. But with the entrepreneurial element gone from my life, a spark was missing.

Most shockingly, I realized I was … kind of depressed.

I began to remember the old cliché about sharks, that they had to keep moving forward or they died. Well, I didn't feel like I was moving forward. Worse, I felt like I wasn't as good of a doctor as I had been. I was certainly taking care of my patients to the best of my ability, but I felt my edge was missing, and I wasn't as personally satisfied with my work.

Eric Thomas has multiple YouTube videos talking about the lion and the gazelle, and one story goes something like this: "Every morning in Africa, a gazelle wakes up. It knows it must run faster than the fastest lion or it will be killed. Every morning a lion wakes up. It knows it must outrun the slowest gazelle or it will starve to death. It doesn't matter whether you're a lion or gazelle. When the sun comes up, you'd better be running if you want to survive." To

Eric's point, are you running toward something in life *or* are you running away from something in life?

During this season of my life, I didn't feel like I was running at all, but if I had to choose, I was probably the gazelle doing the minimum work to be a good physician but not challenging my core being to think in ways to solve problems in a creative fashion.

At first, I couldn't put my finger on what had changed. I knew I loved being a doctor, and I was passionate about following through on my chosen path. But it was like there was a part of me, a big piece of my internal motor, missing. I felt stuck in first gear.

Then I began to check in on USA Staffing. Mark, the guy I had sold the majority interest to, was too busy to really do what I felt was essential to grow the business. So somewhere around the middle of summer in 2014, I began to get involved again with the company, with Mark's blessing. And not because I wanted to but because I thought I had to for the sake of the business and for the sake of me personally.

Much to my surprise, my motor began to rev up again.

The more I worked on the business, the more energized I felt. And, as it had in the past, that energy spilled over into medical work. I could feel my attitude toward my clinical physician practice improving, my patient care excelled, and my creative thinking was in high gear. I felt like the old me but with a renewed sense of duty, energy, and passion.

And that's when I decided I needed to give up the additional medical training in the fellowship due to the fact that I wanted to create a better balance for my time and energy. While I needed to obtain a real physician job to earn an income and still see patients, I also needed to spend more time with USA Staffing Services. My heart knew what it wanted. It wanted me to go ahead and be a practicing doctor and, at the same time, stay deeply involved with my business. It didn't want one or the other.

It wanted both.

GRANTING PERMISSION FOR PASSION

The moral of the story I just related? What you plan in your head doesn't always turn out to be what you want in your heart. Sometimes those two organs get disconnected—and when they do, you can easily get off track. It's easy to overlook the importance of passion if, on paper, it looks like your career trajectory is on course. This is common with all people who feel like their "work" is too important

> **It's easy to overlook the importance of passion if, on paper, it looks like your career trajectory is on course.**

that they can't make time for passion. I use *work* loosely because caregiver burnout with parents and loved ones is real, and I see it often in the hospital setting.

I thought my career was more important than my entrepreneurial passion. When I initially decided to accept the medical fellowship, it was a logical next step in my medical career even though it was optional to actual caring for patients. Part of that logic dictated it was also the time for me to let go of USA Staffing. After all, that was just meant to be a side venture to generate additional income. Logic, however, only gets you so far if it doesn't take into account what you really crave out of life. USA Staffing proved to be much more than a side venture. It had revealed my passion for entrepreneurship, and I couldn't shake it. Without it, the rest of my life felt empty as a result.

I have to admit this was an extremely earthshaking revelation. I have always had a deep passion for patient care, and I value the time I spend attending to those who need medical help. Unfortunately, the life of a physician has less of a patient care component than ever before in the history of medicine. More and more, it's about billing, coding, and dealing with insurance claim disputes. In any given twelve-hour hospital shift, I spend less than two hours actually seeing and talking with patients and the rest of the time sitting in front of the computer filling out forms, writing extremely detailed notes (per insurance company mandates), or arguing on the phone with health insurance companies about the requirement for hospitalization for specific patients. I alluded to this earlier, but the dramatic change from providing care to patients to proving patients are sick to insurance companies has made the entire medical industry a money-focused industry instead of a medical-care-focused industry. This has resulted in a dramatic shift from physicians being able to successfully own their medical practices to nearly eliminating this feature due to the excessive regulation and paperwork-heavy requirements of insurance companies, which call on the administration of an entire hospital to comply with their rules.

While hospital leadership (i.e., nonclinical, nonphysician businesspeople) try to brainwash physicians by saying "insurance claims, notes, and desk work equal patient care," you'd be safe putting down a big fat bet that 99 percent of physicians disagree with that assessment. Still, I wanted to continue in my role as doctor even if that meant I had to put in ten hours of paperwork proving patients are sick for two hours of patient care—as well as go back to running my business. I will talk about how I did this in section 2 of this book when I discuss the huge advantage built into the Zones of Efficiency.

ACKNOWLEDGE AND COMMUNICATE

The upside of passion for your work is that sense of excitement it injects into your professional life and the fact that it creates a natural curiosity or thirst for learning. The downside is … well, you can get a little carried away with it. Or to be more accurate, a *lot* carried away with it. It's like being an addict—you can get to the point where you can't stop yourself and you won't let anybody stand in your way.

I sure didn't. Earlier in this book, I described what happened to me when I had an obsessive mindset that blocked out everything else in my life, including the woman I had just married. Because my first wife was excluded from my emotional life, that union was extremely short lived. That taught me you needed to put some limits on your passion so that it doesn't overwhelm the rest of your life … everything in balance!

All passions have the potential to become an addiction. From a chemical standpoint, there is very little in the brain that distinguishes the rush I get from business from the rush of a runner's high, the butterflies of a new relationship, or the excitement from receiving a new present. They all use very similar dopamine-based and adrenal-based chemical pathways. In the same light, the pathways in the brain that cause addictions can't really distinguish between good addictions and harmful addictions. Taking drugs that give you a high or alcohol that gives you a buzz has real effects on your brain, and a good passion may have the same addiction capacity. You can't talk about passions without acknowledging that almost all of them have a dark side if they're abused. This dark side is highlighted by Tim Grover in his book *Relentless: From Good to Great to Unstoppable*. He talks about the dark side of passion taking over in times of need and argues that having power and control over a passion is what really allows greatness to occur. Painters, musicians, actors, artists, and entrepreneurs can all have separate passions that can contribute to society and add value to their lives, but there are plenty of examples of how these same people can become overrun by the dark side of passion. If they're not kept in check, the risk for addiction, burnout, and self-implosion is real. I'm not just being dramatic, by the way, when I talk about self-implosion. I saw it happen several times to other interns in residency who started taking drugs and drinking to excess or even dropped out because of the stress and pressure.

At first, I failed to keep my passion for entrepreneurship in check. I had to cure myself of my addiction to it in order to find real-life satisfaction. Here's how I did it.

As many of you reading this might already know, Alcoholics Anonymous has a twelve-step program to help alcoholics stop their drinking. Well, I created my own program to help the passionate worker resume a normal, functional personal life. However, being an impatient guy, I didn't have time for twelve steps, so I cut them down to only two. I'm kidding, of course, but the two steps I'm going to reveal laid the groundwork for me to help control the impact of passion and maximize the benefits it brings to my life.

The first step: *acknowledgement.*

My name is Matt, and I have a problem … I'm not going to deny it. As I've already said, spending time on your passions is a selfish activity. After all, your passion is an integral part of your identity, so pursuing it is, yes, egotistical. Is that a bad thing? It can be, but it doesn't have to be. Again, it's not a binary choice. First of all, you have to understand the power of the force that's pushing you forward. Passion may represent a calling, something you feel like you were put on Earth to do, or it may be an activity such as gardening, where you find peace and satisfaction while doing it. In all cases, you typically perform well at the task and find fulfillment in the activity. Your passion can enhance or detract from your life depending on how you handle it. But sometimes you have no idea how to control it because when you first hit on a strong passion, it's impossible to resist.

Before I realized how much entrepreneurship meant to me, I just unconsciously worked night and day without grasping my true motivation. And when you don't understand something, you don't really know how to deal with it. All I knew was I had this incredible drive, and I gave in to it at every turn. I kept thinking I couldn't stop because if I did, my start-up might fall apart and even my work ethic or identity might be questioned. That wasn't true, of course, but my passion for my business overwhelmed common sense.

> **" Life is about mutually beneficial relationships and how you choose to use the time you have to enhance them. "**

When I finally realized I was doing all this work for personal gratification and fulfillment rather than necessity, it was a huge turning point. I understood I had to dedicate a certain amount of time to serve my passion or I would feel unfulfilled, but at the same time, I had to limit it so it wouldn't control my life. I was finally able to explain myself *to* myself, which meant I could start working toward a healthy balance of passion in the context of everything else in my life.

Then I had to explain myself to everyone else.

The second step: *communicate.*

"Dear family and friends, I love being an entrepreneur, and I love being a physician."

I didn't explain myself to my first wife back in 2009 because … well, I didn't get it myself at the time. The result was she grew to resent my all-consuming work hours, and our relationship fell apart. I didn't want that to happen again. I understood it was more important than anything else to keep my loved ones in the loop on what I was doing and why so they could see the big picture as clearly as I did.

During the early days of dating Laura, the old pattern began to happen all over again. I was working way beyond a typical forty-hour week, and she felt like I was gone too much of the time. I didn't really communicate what my objectives were, so she felt hurt. From my standpoint, I wanted to achieve personal satisfaction and fulfillment by following my passion, and I wanted the future "us" to have an exceptional life. Secondly, building this business was going to provide us with a better lifestyle, one that would, for example, allow us to take longer and more luxurious vacations. I put *us* in quotes because my plans were for both of us, but Laura hadn't been aware of that vision because I had failed to explain my motivation to her. I just kept it in my own head.

Maybe I worked more than the average person, but I justified it to myself because we were also going to realize an income that was a lot more than the average person's. That made it worth it in my eyes, and it made sense, but she didn't know that was *why* I was working on the business for so many hours since I never actually told her my thoughts or reasoning. (If you didn't catch this in the previous section, I used the words "in my head," which is not simply a figure of speech in this case. I never actually verbalized to anyone the why or the what behind my long hours.)

Ultimately, after having deeper discussions with her, she understood why I was working such long hours. Still, it took time for her to accept what I had to say and adjust her expectations. Since she accommodated me back then, we are now seeing the benefits of more enjoyable vacations and more control over my schedule, which has allowed flexibility. But more importantly, Laura has been able to realize her passion of being a mother. (She is an amazing mother!) I honestly believe that it is the open communication we had early in our relationship that has allowed our current life to be much more fulfilled both as a couple and individually. I make it a point to carve out significant time alone with Laura and my daughter on a daily basis. Those are the two most precious relationships in my life, and I never want to neglect them.

Adding passion into your life can be difficult, especially when you're in any profession that makes huge demands on your time. If I were a full-time traditional hospital physician, my regular schedule would run from 7:00 a.m. to 7:00 p.m., seven days a week, every other week (a standard schedule for hospital physicians). That would mean I would miss the *entire* day with Hannah fourteen days out of the month (due to the fact that she would be sleeping when I left and when I got back home)—and it would mean that every other weekend I would be unavailable to hang out with my own family. In other words, spending three-fourths of the month as an entrepreneur now allows me to spend *more* time with my family than I would otherwise. My life is more balanced because of my passions, not less.

In section 2, I take the three main components of work, passion, and life and I show you ways to use overlaps to maximize their impact and ultimately increase your Zone of Life Satisfaction.

CHAPTER 3

Life Can Be Summed Up by One Word— Relationships

The good life is built with good relationships.

—Robert J. Waldinger

What's life all about?

Well, the Sunday before I began this part of the book, I was given a sign from above that helped me define it, at least in terms of the theme of achieving balance. Okay, maybe it wasn't exactly from above, but it was pretty close—it came from our minister, Pastor Aaron, who hit me right in the gut with one sentence from his sermon that day: "Life can be defined with one word—*relationships.*"

The truth of that statement resonated with me. All aspects of life are really about nurturing and enjoying relationships with those you love, and these relationships include work relationships, passion-based relationships, and family, friends, and acquaintances. This is why the life circle has overlap in both work and passion as seen in the diagram. Family and friends enrich our days in so many different ways. They add dimensions we can't derive just from what we do for a living. They help us grow and develop as people by taking us beyond our own self-centered concerns and opening us up to new experiences and viewpoints. They also provide the very necessary service of giving us a mental break from our day-to-day grinds.

I'm going to steal another line from that same sermon (is it right to steal from a sermon? I guess Pastor Aaron will let me know!)—a line that perfectly articulates what I was trying to say in the above paragraph: "*The quality of your relationships determines the quantity of your joy.*" Amen, Pastor Aaron.

The key word in that quote is *quality*. Relationships can quickly deteriorate if we don't put in some time and effort in keeping them strong. That's why, to achieve real balance, we must make room for those relationships whenever possible. On a daily basis, I carve out time for my wife, Laura, and daughter, Hannah, every single workday and, for the most part, all the weekend (except for a couple of business calls—I never said I was perfect!). Laura appreciates the effort I make and lets me know she does. That strengthens our relationship tremendously. Laura and Hannah are two important relationships, but there are more relationships that need attention including those with siblings, parents, and neighbors; those within social networks; and even faith-based relationships.

THE IMPORTANCE OF RELATIONSHIPS

It's easy for us to be consumed by either work or passion, especially if those two elements coincide. After all, the former brings us money,

and the latter brings us personal satisfaction, both of which are unde-
niably potent motivators. The problem is that both can easily become
solitary, isolated pursuits. Even though you may love pursuing them,
at the end of the day, you'll still feel as though something major is
missing if you cut yourself off from meaningful relationships. You
will feel incomplete.

This isn't just me talking, by the way. This is the finding of an
enormous body of scientific research that tells us positive human
connection is essential for emotional and physical health, personal
growth, and overall well-being. As a doctor, I've been privy to the
biomedical data that proves healthy relationships are critical to
feeling good about yourself and your life.

One such study, conducted by Brooke Feeney of Carnegie
Mellon University and Nancy Collins of the University of Califor-
nia, Santa Barbara,[3] found that positive relationships are crucial to
offering support for who you are and what you want to accomplish.
They're also a big boost when you find yourself in stressful situations
that might be dragging you down. In the words of Feeney, "Relationships serve an important function of not simply helping people
return to baseline, but helping them to thrive."

Other studies[4] point to five big benefits healthy relationships
provide:

1. **Less stress.** Healthy relationships from marriage to friendship lower the production of cortisol, known as the "stress
   hormone." Married or paired people are more able to fend

---

3   Douglas LaBier, "Why Positive Relationships Are Needed for
     Emotional Health," *Psychology Today*, September 26, 2014, https://
     www.psychologytoday.com/us/blog/the-new-resilience/201409/
     why-positive-relationships-are-needed-emotional-health.

4   Northwestern Medicine, "Five Benefits of Healthy Relationships," https://www.
     nm.org/healthbeat/healthy-tips/5-benefits-of-healthy-relationships.

off the pressures of life because of their constant and mutual support of each other.

2. **Healing power.** A strong relationship can actually help you bounce back more quickly from sickness. Research suggests married people who undergo heart surgery are three times more likely to survive the first three months after surgery than a single patient. They are also a lot more confident about recovering from illness or a medical procedure.

3. **Healthier behaviors.** People in relationships tend to look out for each other and promote healthier behavior, such as better diets, more exercise, and so on, because they want their partners to experience well-being. These behaviors aren't always fun, so having someone rooting for you can make a big difference. This also has a huge impact in work relationships with colleagues. I have seen my employees take walks together, eat lunch together, and even manage stress together, and they ultimately support each other in trying (most times) to make healthy decisions.

4. **A greater sense of purpose.** Healthy relationships make you feel needed and like you're a part of something bigger than yourself. They give you a sense of purpose, and that sense of purpose can actually add years to your life. In family relationships there may be long-term family goals such as working toward retirement or a vacation. In a work setting, the relationship between employees has the power of enhancing the corporate mission, and church relation-ships allow people to experience God and/or a higher level of being and destination.

5. **A longer life.** And speaking of adding years to your life,

research also shows healthy social relationships contribute mightily to preventing an early death, more so than such generally known common sense steps such as taking blood pressure medication or avoiding exposure to pollution. But what about when social relationships are lacking? Well, one study[5] says this has the same effect on your health as smoking fifteen cigarettes a day! The study also reported that low levels of social interaction put you at the same health risk as an alcoholic, are more harmful than not exercising, and are twice as harmful as obesity.

Yes, take it from me, Dr. Kolinski—not having relationships is *very* harmful to your health! Notice that in nearly all cases, the benefits of having *any* relationships allows for higher quality of life even if they are predominately friendships or community-based relationships. Ultimately, the stronger the relationships, the higher the associated benefits, but strong and healthy relationships can include those with coworkers, neighbors, significant others, and friends.

GOING BEYOND YOURSELF

The life section of your balancing act differs from work and passion in one very important way: it's not just about you. Relationships must be a two-way street in order to be healthy ones.

Passion, as I've noted, is intrinsically selfish, as you are pursuing what fulfills *you*. Work is mostly a one-way street in a selfless way. For example, you have to do what the boss wants you to do, or you might be taking that one-way street right out the door. Relationships that

---

5   Laura Trowbridge, "Study: Lack of Friends Is Like Smoking 15 Cigs a Day Health Wise," *Digital Journal*, August 7, 2010, http://www.digitaljournal.com/article/295653#ixzz5poBezdxm.

are only occurring in the life section are about (or at least should be about) a give-and-take interaction. You're interacting with people other than yourself or someone you work with/for. And you're committing to those interactions because you want to develop those mutually beneficial relationships. It is finding joy in the discovery of a person outside of yourself *and* sharing personal information with others who don't already know you. Examples of relationships that solely remain in the life section include the following: those with a spouse/significant other, parents, siblings, college friends, friends from the community (not associated with passion or your job), neighbors, and so on.

> **I ended up having to consciously choose to make time for my relationships and grow them, instead of leaving them to wither and die.**

I myself had to learn the value of that kind of two-way street. When I was locked into just the work and passion sections of my life, it left me feeling a little empty. I ended up having to consciously choose to make time for my relationships and grow them, instead of leaving them to wither and die. The difference since then has been profound and has enriched my life in a variety of ways.

But for now let's go back to the research, which tells us relationships work best when you're able to accept support from those around you as well as offer it when needed. The use of support can also be applied to taking the time to listen and get to know someone on a deeper level because sometimes the support they are looking for is simply being acknowledged as a human being. The secret is to create mutually caring connections because this enables you (and the people you connect with) to grow emotionally and achieve more than you would have otherwise. When you just expect a friend to do all the heavy lifting in the relationship, that friend grows resentful and may even disappear from your life. The same bad feelings develop on your end when you feel like you're the only one who puts in all the work.

Someone once told me about a friend who kept calling him every other night, keeping him on the phone for an hour or so to continually discuss a problematic romantic relationship. At first, he was happy to lend an ear and help out. But then, as the calls kept coming every other night, he noticed this friend kept describing the same issues over and over and never seemed to be doing anything to resolve the situation. Worse, this so-called friend never asked him how *he* was doing, even though this person was eating up hours and hours of his time. Finally, he had to gently tell his friend that he didn't have the time to keep going over the same ground night after night—it was cutting into his time with his family. The friend was indignant, hung up ... and they never spoke again.

The above is the very definition of an unhealthy relationship, the kind you neither want nor need. So how do you successfully create mutually caring connections? Here are a few tips on how you can do your part.

- **Listen.** When a friend or loved one has a problem, they're not always asking you to solve it. Frequently, they're just asking for your time. Just allowing them to get something off their chest can be therapeutic for them. And who knows? Maybe you do have the answer! Of course, you don't want to get in an endless loop as my friend did in the story I just related. But if their situation is genuinely serious, you will definitely want to give more than you receive during that difficult time.

- **Communicate openly and without judgment.** When you *are* listening, it's important not to blame the other person or make them feel worse about their situation. Lead with questions, not judgments, and make room for them to answer honestly and openly. If they have screwed up, they'll usually admit it, and that will open the door to a frank discussion. Also, when you have good news to share, it means a lot to people when you communicate the good news with them personally because this allows them to share in your successes. Sharing wins with each other oftentimes allows you to take a mediocre relationship and enhance it.

- **Trust and respect each other.** Relationships are hard to sustain when one person involved doesn't really trust or believe in the other. The situation is worse when both people behave this way. When you feel like you're being lied to or regularly disrespected, it's not a good sign, and this usually means you're in a relationship that won't survive. Trust and respect are essential to the glue of a solid relationship, and this glue is something that needs to be reinforced continuously. Spreading rumors or sharing private knowledge breaks both trust and respect.

- **Make time for each other.** This is critical. Most relationships fall apart due to simple neglect. Most people in my life understand when I'm crazy busy because that's a big part of my entrepreneurial life. But I've learned some coping skills that enable me to make time for relationships even while I'm heavily involved in the work-passion circles. Also, note one big exception to this rule: there are people we form such strong and solid relationships with early in our lives (childhood and school friends are a good example) that it doesn't really matter how often you talk with or email them. You can always pick up right where you left off and swap the same bad jokes you told ten years ago (e.g., the quarter joke and the 7-Eleven joke—shout out to my Columbia Avenue roommates!).

On this last point, I'm proud that my relationships with my friends from college are still in existence. Those connections have such a strong foundation that, to this day, I believe they know me almost better than anyone else. And that's helpful when I need a reality check. They quickly sense when I'm not quite acting like myself, so they're some of the first people to ask me what's going on. It's comforting to have people like that in my life who know me inside out—and whom I can lean on when I need support.

PERSONAL TIME AND REFLECTION

While the life portion of your schedule is mostly about attending to mutually beneficial relationships, occasionally you have to focus on creating a mutually beneficial relationship with yourself. What does that mean? It means putting in some time taking care of yourself so that you can not only enjoy your life space to the fullest but also your work and passion spaces.

If you don't look after yourself, all kinds of bad stuff can happen—and probably will. For instance, if you go nonstop 24/7 with work or even partying, you can get physically rundown and even sick, you can burn out your mental engine and completely lose your mojo, or you can even lose track of who you are and what you're doing with your life.

When you regularly practice self-care, however, you're making the best version of yourself possible. You become healthier, stronger, and more able to mentally take on the toughest challenges. It can be hard with the hectic pace of today's world to make time for yourself—

but that hectic pace is exactly *why* you need to make that time. This is different than the selfish part of the passion section because in your relationship with yourself, you are going to force yourself to eat veggies, take vitamins, and exercise … none of which are typically part of someone's passions or hobbies. If you don't pay attention to your physical and mental health, you'll find yourself falling backward instead of moving forward.

To the best of my ability, I try not to miss my morning routine of the Miracle Morning, created by Hal Elrod, every weekday. This routine includes a combination of silence, reflection, and emotional recalibration. I make it happen at a time when nobody is going to interrupt me (theoretically, anyway). That's time for just me—so I make sure it's also a time that doesn't conflict with any other area of my life. When you manage your time correctly, you'll be able to make room for self-care, and you should. It's how you refuel, allowing you to give more energy to the areas of life, work, or passion that need your attention for the day.

It can be tough to push yourself to do it. For example, most people (I'm no exception) really don't look forward to exercising. Once you commit to it, though, you'll discover that physical activity actually activates the brain's pleasure circuit and leaves you with a mental high. Other health benefits include improvements in the function of the cardiovascular, pulmonary, and endocrine systems. Voluntary exercise is also connected to long-term improvements in mental function and, amazingly, is the single best thing you can do to slow the cognitive decline that accompanies normal aging. It also blunts the brain's response to physical and emotional stress. When you combine the physical exercise with meditation, the benefits are even more impressive. Vishen Lakhiani, author of *The Code of the Extraordinary Mind*, puts it like this:

If you were doing this exercise 150 years ago, everyone around you would have stunk. Back then, we didn't have the practice of a daily shower. We weren't trained to brush our teeth. Cologne and perfume were mostly used by the very wealthy. Deodorant didn't exist. In the 1900s, humanity simply got used to its own stinking smell.

Today we do all kinds of things in the morning to clean and prepare our bodies for the day. We brush, shower, spray on cologne, and dress well, all to keep our physical bodies fresh and clean. Yet billions of us wake up each morning feeling worry, stress, anxiety, and fear and don't do anything about it. We assume this is normal, but it's not. Just as we can wash our bodies, so we can have systems to completely "wash" our minds of these debilitating feelings.

Self-care is about knowing what you should do to take care of yourself, which, in turn, enables you to feel strong enough to take care of others as well. It's another important key to keeping your balancing act intact. That's why I've found that self-care needs to be an active choice, not something you hope you get around to one of these days (which invariably turns out to be *none* of these days).

Here's a quick checklist of self-care tasks everyone should keep in mind to enhance the life circle:

- **Pursue a nutritious and healthy diet.**

- **Get enough sleep.** Seven to eight hours a night is recommended for most adults.

- **Exercise.** Of course.

- **Get regular checkups with your doctor and dentist.** If you feel your mental health is suffering, seek a professional to help you sort it out. No shame in that.

- **Find ways to relax your mind.** Meditate or do yoga if you find it benefits you. You may find one or the other helps you clear your mind and gain a new perspective on your life.

- **Just say no—sometimes.** For example, I try to unplug from my phone when spending time with my family. Likewise, avoid so-called obligations that you don't enjoy, don't need to do, and just take time away from the rest of your life rather than adding anything substantial to it.

At the beginning of this chapter, I asked the question, "What's life all about?" Here's my answer: Life is about mutually beneficial relationships and how you choose to use the time you have to enhance them. This may occur as part of family time, volunteer work, religion, hobbies, social get-togethers, and so forth. All these kinds of life relationships yield even bigger rewards when they intersect with your circles of work and passion. These create Zones of Efficiency that enable you to share what you love with other like-minded individuals.

The Zones of Efficiency

CHAPTER 4

What Are Zones of Efficiency, and Why Are They Important?

In chapter 1, I introduced the idea of Zones of Efficiency, which is where two areas of Work-Passion-Life Balance overlap. This notion has allowed me to achieve more satisfaction while at the same time improving my life fulfillment by combining parts of my life and maximizing my time to create the equilibrium I craved and needed.

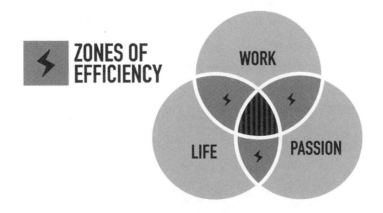

The only thing in my way was giving myself permission to create a plan that allowed me to achieve all my desires while ensuring I maintained the key relationships in my life. Specifically, I had to *allow* myself to seek out passion in my work, and that meant I didn't have to force myself to choose a medical career over entrepreneurship—I could do both! Using the three Zones of Efficiency as demonstrated above would, in turn, bring me the highest overall life satisfaction.

> **Specifically, I had to allow myself to seek out passion in my work, and that meant I didn't have to force myself to choose a medical career over entrepreneurship—I could do both!**

And that's been the case since I put my plan in action.

I'll admit it's an unconventional choice. You don't meet many doctors, especially younger ones, who are running nonmedical businesses when they're not on their hospital rounds. However, almost 100 percent of my physician partners *wish* they were running their own business, even if it was a medical one. From my discussions with my peers, it seems as though having the ambition to become a doctor signals an underlying desire to be an entrepreneur. That could be a carryover from an earlier time since most physicians up until the early 2000s were independent business owners and not employees paid by a hospital or clinic. This interaction between people's jobs and passions is a clear sign that there is both an opportunity for efficiency and a separation of work from passion at times. The same can be said for the other two Zones of Efficiency as seen in the diagram. When you overlap work and life or life and passion, you maximize your time and effort and can achieve more satisfaction and fulfillment.

I encourage everyone who is reading this book to evaluate their current divisions of life and use the next few chapters to think about ways to maximize overlap. The benefits will be multiplied and will ultimately increase the Zone of Life Satisfaction, which is shown below.

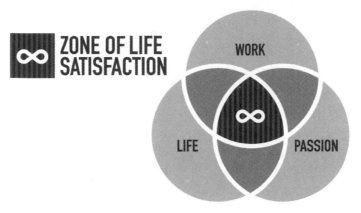

Zone of Life Satisfaction: this is a result of having increased balance and overlap between work, life, and passion. This visualization shows that the more overlap you have, the more balanced you are. This is the result of creating large zones of efficiencies between each aspect of your life and maximizing your life to the fullest.

Now, a Zone of Efficiency isn't magical. It doesn't mean when you're in it that you won't feel weighted down by the obligations of the two zones involved (i.e., the work-passion, life-passion, or work-life zones)—even a dream job has its dull and dreary side. For example, at my business, I'm not exactly fond of creating budgets, talking to banks about increasing my credit line, or dealing with workers' comp issues; however, these are all elements of my company that are crucial to its success, so I follow through on them in order to gain the benefits of running the business. On the other hand, I actually love making sales calls because that's how you grow your revenue and your business. More importantly, I have the opportunity to talk with other entrepreneurs and develop relationships during those calls and, hopefully, solve one of their current operational issues.

Overall, however, work combined with passion brings a

much higher sense of fulfillment. Meanwhile, I have developed some wonderful friendships within the entrepreneurial world that maximize the joy I feel due to the combined life-passion zone. Lastly, I have been fortunate to have a wonderful partnership with Mark Curtiss that has added value to me and my family personally, which is a great example of how the work-life zone can truly enhance both aspects when combined. The Zone of Life Satisfaction requires that all three Zones of Efficiency be maximized; that is, the only way to increase your Zone of Life Satisfaction is to increase the Zones of Efficiency.

That, however, can bring its own problems.

The area where there is overlap between all three circles is the Zone of Life Satisfaction. The larger the overlap, the better balance, more fulfillment, and higher level of satisfaction you'll get from your life. You don't need to be an entrepreneur to achieve a large Zone of Life Satisfaction. By acknowledging the three areas and working to increase the Zones of Efficiency, you will naturally grow your Zone of Life Satisfaction. While entrepreneurs may have an advantage when it comes to increasing their Zone of Life Satisfaction, they are only one group of people with a common passion. While I can give several examples of nonentrepreneurs, I would like to share with you the person who has helped me find greater balance in my own life, someone who has been an example of how life should be lived.

> **You don't need to be an entrepreneur to achieve a large Zone of Life Satisfaction.**

This person who has been my role model is my wife, Laura, and her passion is caregiving. She is a nurse by training, which means she is a natural caregiver, and it has always been a trait that I have admired about her. Before we had Hannah, she was a bedside nurse. She was an exceptional nurse with several nursing friends, and she generally enjoyed working in the hospital most days. When we were working the home care business together, which I'll go into later, she developed amazing customer relationships with the elderly people of our community and excelled when creating care plans and connecting with other franchise owners in a similar area. Most recently, when we had our daughter, she transitioned to caring for our daughter, and again she has continued to grow in this role to be an amazing mother who is constantly learning and working to provide the best education, experience, and life for Hannah. She has developed a social network in every phase of her life and has found people who share her interests and desire to help others. This group of wonderful moms calls themselves "MOST," which stands for "Mothers of South Tampa." They have a thriving Facebook group that is very inclusive, although you must live in the South Tampa area to join. In this case, as a full-time mother, she has several large Zones of Efficiency between the passion-life, passion-work, and work-life areas, which leads to a large Zone of Life Satisfaction and appears to help her balance her life despite the stresses of raising a young child.

I am sure each of you reading this book can identify someone who is an excellent caregiver, and maybe that person has cared for you in one aspect of your life or another. On the other hand, I know each of you can also identify a full-time mother or father who may not have enjoyed being a full-time caregiver. In the second situation, they probably did a good job raising kids, but their life balance may not have been optimized due to the fact that their passion may have been something such as sales or finance. However, due to the family's situation, they needed to become a full-time mother or homemaker.

This person is typically the one who jumps back into work as soon as the child goes to school all day, and at that point they feel they are living a more balanced and fulfilled life. I can use myself as an example. If I needed to become a full-time dad, I would do it for the sake of my family, but since my major passion is entrepreneurship and patient care is my second passion, I would probably be dreaming up new businesses during Hannah's nap time. And I would put them on the shelf until she was older if I wasn't able to make the time to spend on these businesses. In this example, since caregiving isn't my core passion, I probably wouldn't be networking with other parents or reading the latest caregiving trends on fun projects for long car rides or crafts to do on a plane, but Laura definitely does, and she has a natural curiosity that is truly breathtaking. It drives her desire to be an excellent caregiver and mother. Even though many people may disagree, I consider full-time parents to have one of the hardest jobs, but when passion is included, they make it look easy!

Over the next few chapters I will go into more explanations of the various ways to enhance your Zones of Efficiency, which will lead to benefits in all areas of life.

CHAPTER 5

Zone of Efficiency 1

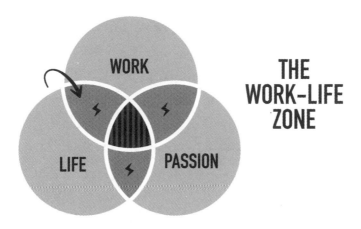

"All work and no play makes Jack a dull boy."

Most of you have heard that proverb in the past. But I'd like to offer my own version: "All work and no play makes Jack an *unbalanced* boy." Or perhaps I should just swap it out for the phrase I heard frequently from my colleagues while in medical school and later when working endless shifts in residency: "Work hard, play hard!"

You may be lucky enough to have found a way to combine passion with your work, as I discussed in the last chapter. But if you don't make room to also honor your personal relationships, you will slowwwwly find yourself losing touch with your social circles, even your family life. Eventually, you'll find the only things you can talk about are what happened during your work hours and the weather. You'll grow increasingly one dimensional and isolated—and that will eventually catch up with you. (This actually happens to most medical students because of the enormous amount of time, mental energy, and compassion we need to apply during training. We typically lose touch with reality and with our outside relationships.)

It's not fun to go through something like that, but it can be funny to watch it happen. If you've ever seen the Michael Keaton comedy *Multiplicity*, you know what I'm talking about. Keaton's character has a hard time juggling his work and family life and creates several identical clones of himself (okay, it's not a true-life story) so each one can assume full-time responsibility of a different aspect of his life. Soon, however, those clones become far from identical.

> **When you put everything into one part of your life, the other parts can't help but suffer. And you can't help but suffer as a result.**

"Work Michael Keaton" gradually becomes less emotional and more task-oriented—while "Family Michael Keaton" transforms into a traditional housewife type, focused on the kids, taking care of the home, and bemoaning the lack of emotional support from Work Michael Keaton. So even though both Michael Keatons begin as the exact same guy, they evolve into completely different individuals with different agendas because they're dedicated to different responsibilities. And soon both have absolutely *no* understanding of what the other wants from them.

Quite frankly, it's funny because it's true. When you put everything into one part of your life, the other parts can't help but suffer.

And *you* can't help but suffer as a result. Maximizing the Zone of Efficiency between work and life ultimately means developing relationships with work colleagues outside of work hours, which will allow you to have a deeper connection when you are actually working together. Adding personal relationships in the workplace needs to come with some barriers, but when done well, it can enhance both your personal life and your work life. At the same time, it is important to accept the fact that work and life are separate for a reason. If you have a hard time separating the two, instead of maximizing efficiency, you can develop a work circle that dominates, resulting in a shrinking life circle. You have to protect the integrity of both work and life while at the same time looking for ways to maximize overlap in a healthy manner, and that sometimes means building boundaries.

BUILDING WALLS UP

Imagine you're at your parents' home for dinner and you get a work call. Imagine you spend half the night on that work call. Now imagine how unimportant your parents will be left feeling after you've basically ignored them in their own house.

I've been guilty of that kind of bad behavior (sorry, Mom and Dad), and sometimes I would be at a restaurant with friends and take a call I felt was too important to miss. I realize now that most of the time, I didn't *have* to take that call, but back then I didn't have that kind of maturity. The result was I would spend most of the time during what was supposed to be a social occasion attending strictly to business by sending texts and emails or making other calls to deal with a company situation.

I allowed my work to overwhelm my life. And that meant I was doing the people in my life a disservice, especially if I was interrupting something special, such as a holiday or birthday celebration, with business concerns that probably could have been dealt with the next day. I wasn't giving my relationships with family and friends the time they deserved. I was indirectly telling them my work was more important than they were, and I didn't even realize I was sabotaging those precious relationships.

So I had to learn to reprioritize. That effort really began in earnest when Laura and I took our honeymoon. For a whole week, I kept my cell phone off. Yes, I may have twitched a bit with tension from going cold turkey for that long, but it was well worth the effort. Thus, powering down the iPhone is now something I do when I feel it's appropriate. For example, recently, I had the phone off for all of Mother's Day—that way, my wife can see for herself that she's more important than anything else in my life.

That's a message I continue to try to send any way I can. That's why when I'm working at USA Staffing Services, I make every effort to leave by 6:00 p.m. If it was just me that was involved, if I didn't have a family, I could easily stay at the office for many more hours. Time spent at the office tends to feel like playtime at my business, and it's hard to cut your fun and games short. But it was something I knew I needed to do for Laura. She requested this, and I listened and obeyed—because my new approach to life is to prioritize relationships, and ours is my most important one.

You don't have to allow your work to overwhelm your personal life. When your smartphone starts buzzing in your pocket or purse, you don't have to fish it out and see who's after you about what. Once you've committed to spending time with friends, family, or children, they should be your priority when you're with them. Yes, emergencies can happen, and they'll understand when such situations take you away. What they won't understand is if you end up on the phone endlessly, discussing something trivial that can easily be tackled during work hours. Trust me, I know. I've been that guy, and I have made that mistake more times than I care to admit.

Because I understand my patterns, I've become increasingly vigilant about maintaining boundaries. I've evolved to understand what's important and what's not important in the moment. Insignificant things can obviously be put off—and even something significant can be handled more quickly and efficiently if you put the right systems in place.

If you can't make the people who are closest to you feel important, those relationships are going to suffer and possibly even disintegrate, which means your life circle will become smaller overall. That's not necessary, and it's certainly not desirable, not when it only takes a little time and effort to honor those relationships. For example, when I'm in Tampa, I devote roughly four hours of every weekday to my wife and daughter and nearly the entire weekend when possible. When you consider the fact that I'm also spending eight hours of that day at my business, those four hours don't seem like so much—but given my busy schedule, it shows Laura and Hannah how much I care. It's all a matter of perspective. Honestly, they have such a busy social schedule with other moms, zoo trips, and aquarium trips that they seem to not mind the disproportionate time as long as it is quality time. I have to ensure that those hours are not bogged down by text messages, emails, or phone calls because then I might as well be at the office instead of at home.

> **If you can't make the people who are closest to you feel important, those relationships are going to suffer and possibly even disintegrate, which means your life circle will become smaller overall.**

TAKING WALLS DOWN

Sometimes, instead of putting up walls between your personal and professional spaces, it's useful to knock them completely down to maximize the Zone of Efficiency between the two as long as it is done with vigilance and good intention.

One of my key strategies to maintain a strong Zone of Efficiency between work and life is to overlap the time spent in both areas if possible. Opportunities such as developing personal relationships with work colleagues outside of work hours is a simple way to enhance the zone between work and life. Another way to achieve this is by involving family members or close friends in business ventures and/or finding them a job at the same company. The end result is the same in both situations: developing a network of relationships that are involved in both your personal life and your work life, which maximizes your Zone of Efficiency between the two. As an entrepreneur and business owner, when there's an opportunity to merge work with my private life, I take it, and oftentimes this translates to hiring friends and family. I have had the pleasure of working with my wife, my mom, and my cousin during various business ventures over the past several years, and there are both success stories and hard lessons learned from these experiences. I wouldn't change my decisions because ultimately they have all made me a better businessperson, but in some cases feelings were hurt or relationships suffered due to the employee-employer relationship that was initiated. Sometimes walls between family and work are needed, simply because you have to recognize the other person's wants and needs, but in many cases, with open communication you can find a way to work with family members or close friends.

For example, after Laura and I moved to Tampa, she said maybe she'd like to try running her own business with my help so she could share in what I loved to do. To me, this idea seemed like a godsend—we could spend more time together and possibly create a new success story at the same time. So together with my business partner Mark Curtiss, we invested in a franchise called Synergy Home Care. It was a business my wife, who was a nurse, knew something about, and it felt like it would allow us to mash up our work, life, and passion into one big ball of profitable fun!

However, my entrepreneurial mindset kicked into overdrive with this start-up—I couldn't stop thinking about how to grow our new business even when Laura and I were just spending time together. We might start talking about what we were going to have for dinner and then suddenly, my brain would completely veer off into another direction. "Hey," I'd say out of nowhere, "I thought of a new marketing strategy for Synergy. Want to hear about it?"

Well, unless it was during our official work hours, it turned out she *didn't* want to hear about it!

For instance, when I brought up Synergy on a Saturday, it would bring her down. It was the weekend, and she wanted to relax and forget about it for a while. When I reminded her about it, it just brought an unneeded shot of stress back into her life. She wanted a firm separation between the time we spent working on the business and the time we spent alone together. From her perspective, Synergy was her job and not her passion. Not long after starting the business, it was clear that what I called passion, she called work, and this caused some strain in our relationship.

I still had a problem because I couldn't stop myself from thinking about it, so I came up with a simple solution: when I had a thought about Synergy during our "off hours," I just made a note about it without saying a word to Laura, and then I could bring it up when we were back in our Synergy offices on Monday morning, working on the business.

Ultimately, we actually worked well together when it came to strictly the job and the business, but the problem was she didn't share my entrepreneurial passion about Synergy. We didn't know until we actually started working on the business that the difference between the level of passion we had about it would ultimately be the challenge we would face. That's completely fine—you can't know if you like something until you try it. She had to find out for herself that entrepreneurship wasn't for her, just like I had to find out for myself that only being a doctor wasn't enough for me. We learn a lot about ourselves from our own experiences if we're open to it—we then just have to be smart enough to take that valuable knowledge into account when we move forward.

In the end, we worked well together, but the difference in passion was the core reason why we struggled with this venture. Just because it didn't work for us doesn't mean it can't work with you and your significant other—there are quite a few high-profile couples who *do* end up working side by side, sharing the same work passion. Jay-Z and Beyoncé are just one famous couple who do projects together, as well as apart. The actress Melissa McCarthy often stars in movies written and directed by her husband. And now that Bill Gates no longer runs Microsoft, he and his wife, Melinda, devote their professional lives to charitable endeavors. It *can* work if both of you are on the same page about your passions. And if actual work is too much of a barrier, you can volunteer with friends and family or do work around the house together.

But what if you don't have anyone in your personal life who shares an interest in your work? What if you don't have anyone to talk to who understands what you go through at the office or wherever you happen to work?

As I've expressed elsewhere in this book, almost all my social friends and family don't understand why I enjoy running a business, and the work part of running the business is more complicated at times. Even though I try to explain the stress or frustrations, many people still don't get it—simply because they don't share the same enthusiasms. I personally struggle at times when building relationships with employees even though I truly respect and cherish the team that I've put together. It's difficult to have a real, heartfelt relationship with someone who works for you or someone you work for due to the power dynamic that gets in the way of having a completely open and honest relationship.

Fortunately, as part of the USA Staffing Services Authorized Dealer program, we work with independently owned and operated recruitment firms throughout the country. In the early years, I struggled to find people in my social network who knew the frustrations of running a staffing or recruiting business; however, the authorized dealers allowed me to increase my Zone of Efficiency between work and life. In many ways I was able to connect on a social level and on a work level with the authorized dealers in my network because they are all business owners themselves. I developed a social network of peers, and we worked together to help grow the business. My early relationships with people such as Adrian Bell, owner of Hosted Records; Ronalyn, owner of Oxford Legal Group; and Steve Askew, owner of Digital Staffing Age, are what have allowed me to mature in my experience, develop programs that benefited them, and grow the business. As a result of these early relationships in the work setting, I was able to expand USA Staffing Services to the point where we made the famous Inc. 500 list four years in a row. As the Zone of Efficiency grew, my work-based successes grew as well.

CHAPTER 6

Zone of Efficiency 2

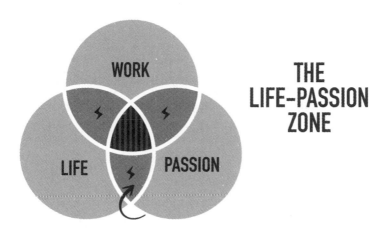

THE
LIFE-PASSION
ZONE

At the beginning, I was a very lonely entrepreneur. I began that journey without much outside support. My parents certainly didn't get it—after all, my dad had spent the majority of his entire professional career at two companies. They were always rooting for me but concerned about this choice.

You might ask, What about the people I worked with? Couldn't I lean on them a little for some understanding? Not always. Even though I've had partners and employees along the way (and still do), because they were entangled in my companies, I couldn't really have the frank and open conversations with them that I yearned for. I must say I did bond with many of the one hundred or so entre-preneurs a year I ended up talking to when I was primarily selling our Authorized Dealer program to recruiting companies. But again, because I was out to do business with those entrepreneurs, the inter-actions didn't create the kinds of relationships where I could discuss my own work issues with them.

The result? I was mostly on my own in terms of navigating important business issues and working through big decisions. Finally, in 2015, all that changed after I won my first Inc. 500 award.

For those of you who aren't familiar with the Inc. 500, it's awarded annually by *Inc.* magazine to the 500 fastest-growing private companies in the United States. I was ecstatic when USA Staffing Services made it to number 310 on the list in 2015. What was even more amazing is the fact that there is also an Inc. 5000—and I jumped right past those other 4,500 companies to land in the top 500.

It instantly changed everything and filled a void I had been feeling for years. I was suddenly validated in the eyes of my parents as well as many of my friends who didn't understand being a doctor wasn't enough for me and would ask why the heck I was spending all this time trying to get a staffing business off the ground when I was a licensed physician. Now, they finally saw I was not only running a legitimate business but a successful one, and they were suddenly giving me all the high fives I could handle.

I was also proud of the fact that I was contributing to the economy of the United States of America, as well as making a dent in the unemployment figures. That gave me more confidence in moving forward. It didn't feel like a crazy risk anymore; it felt like the real deal. And that put me over a major hump in my personal life.

But that wasn't the best part of winning that award. No, the real rewards began when I attended the Inc. 500 awards ceremony.

That's when I discovered I truly was no longer alone.

WHEN THE PROFESSIONAL TURNS PERSONAL

USA Staffing Services had been in existence for five years when we finally received the Inc. 500 award and, as I said, up until then, I had felt fairly isolated in my entrepreneurial role—there was nobody with whom I could fully share my business's ups and downs. At the awards, however, I met all these other entrepreneurs who were just like me and thought like me. They had the same *passion* as me. It was like I had finally stumbled into my own tribe.

This was a huge aha moment. Now, I no longer felt different and isolated. Instead, I was part of a community and a successful one at that. There were hundreds of people at the ceremony, and all of us were all celebrating each other's wins. This was huge and exciting—a game changer. And things were about to get even more amazing.

I was introduced to Laura Webb, who was a member of the Tampa, Florida, chapter of the Entrepreneurs' Organization. "Entrepreneurs' Organization?" I thought to myself. "You mean there's a *club* for people like me? And it's in the city where I live?" It was too good to be true. Locally, there was a large group of like-minded individuals I could interact with monthly, weekly, even daily if I wanted to. I quickly joined up and ended up very happy I did because it added a lot of value to my life and quickly expanded my Zone of Efficiency between life and passion.

After joining, I had people who would help celebrate my wins, pick me up when I was struggling, and give me advice: business owner to business owner, entrepreneur to entrepreneur, all in a helpful and nonjudgmental way. This newfound network and number of companions added significant value to my life. One of the core features of the EO is the use of gestalt iterations where we focus more on sharing similar experiences rather than telling each other what to do. Suddenly, I was able to have conversations about my business that other EO members could understand because they had been through the same kinds of experiences.

My EO experience has evolved to the point where I now sit on the board of directors for the local chapter, and I am involved with regional and global leaders with the same passion. Now, on a monthly basis, a close-knit group of us EO entrepreneurs get together to brainstorm about our personal, business, and financial issues. We serve as each other's personal boards of directors and give each other the kind of perspective and advice we would be hard pressed to find elsewhere.

For me, this became the perfect junction of life and passion because over the past four years, I have developed mutually beneficial relationships with people who share the same passion as me. These organizations exist for other passions/hobbies/interests, and the use of Facebook and LinkedIn has helped to improve the presence of these organizations. I mentioned this earlier, but for mothers living in South Tampa, the Facebook group MOST (Mothers of South Tampa) has

> **When you're able to talk openly with people who completely understand your passion and the why for what you do, you end up learning more about yourself.**

become *the place* for them to connect with other mothers, seek advice, and share experiences.

My EO relationships have helped me continue to develop my

company and refine my entrepreneurial passion by inspiring me to explore new and better ways to do business, but ultimately, adding people with a similar passion to my social network is what has made the biggest difference. When you're able to talk openly with people who completely understand your passion and the *why* for what you do, you end up learning more about yourself. New interests are sparked, along with new ideas and new approaches to doing traditional tasks.

I learned a huge lesson about maintaining my own personal balancing act through the process of becoming involved in a professional association. I only wished I had availed myself of this opportunity before—but I was too accustomed to seeing my entrepreneurship as a solitary pursuit. I didn't get how genuine, quality life relationships, the kind I discussed in the last chapter, could connect to what I did for a living.

Now I do.

Building strong personal relationships with others who have the same passion for running businesses brought down a big wall between my work and my life. It is important to note that this is a passion-based group and not a specialty professional group (such as the American Staffing Association or the Florida Staffing Association, both of which I am also a part of). The ASA and FSA are important professional groups, but for me, USA Staffing is one of the ways I express my entrepreneurial passion. And the more walls you can tear down between the three circles of your life, the more easily you can achieve balance. Forging strong personal relationships with your peers creates a passion and life overlap that can provide the kind of support, energy, and experience-backed inspiration that renews your commitment and refreshes your spirit.

THE PRESCRIPTION FOR LIFE–PASSION SATISFACTION

The funny thing is I actually experienced this kind of Zone of Efficiency earlier in my life, but because it was based in medicine and was a very informal and casual relationship, I never really applied it to my entrepreneurial pursuits until I joined the EO.

It happened in medical school. A friend of mine, Dr. Shilpan Patel, and I were both dissatisfied with how the business model for doctors was rapidly changing at the time, evolving from doctors owning private practices to being employed by large hospital corporations. As a result, we began discussing business more than medicine, brainstorming sometimes all day about ways to improve the medical industry and address some of its flaws. We would start from the standpoint of, If we were in charge, how would we make it better?

This, of course, triggered my obsession with solving problems—he had the same preoccupation—so when we got together, that's what we would talk about. It was a preview of my EO relationships to come in that we were peers, at the same level, and in the same situation. We were facing the same daunting professional challenges but also had a passion for fixing the broken medical system at that time.

To this day, he's still someone I talk with on a regular basis. He's rising in the ranks in the hospital system, and he's currently the chief medical informatics officer of a hospital in Chicago and is now learning how he can have an impact on the hospital, community, and patients by optimizing technology. It's incredible to see him become a decision maker on issues we talked about ten-plus years ago. It is gratifying to know we helped each other realize our potentials—and, again, it happened through the kind of personal relationship that started in medical school as a coworker type of relationship that ultimately developed into a strong personal friendship with a common passion. Since we don't work in the same hospital, we technically aren't coworkers; however, we remain friends with similar passions for problem-solving and improving the healthcare system, which fits perfectly in the Zone of Efficiency between life and passion.

So if you haven't already, think about seeking out some relationships based on your passion that can also satisfy you

> **So if you haven't already, think about seeking out some relationships based on your passion that can also satisfy you on a personal level.**

on a personal level. Here are some of the benefits you can realize from these kinds of associations:

- **Professional development within your passion.** One of the best ways to enhance your own personal knowledge and keep up with your passion is to attend conferences or professional development meetings. It's in everyone's interest to stay current with business trends and how you should be evolving with them—so the value of sharing the latest developments and how everyone is reacting to them can't be underestimated. These types of groups exist for hundreds of passion-based organizations and in formal associations, such as the EO. They will also typically hold regular educational meetings and talks that will provide useful updates and perspectives on issues that affect the topics you are most passionate about.

- **Networking.** Networking with like-minded individuals

not only enhances your Zone of Efficiency between life and passion but may also help with finding a job that pays you for your passion. The relationships and discussions that you will have when networking will surely lead you to some interesting opportunities.

- **Mentorship.** Whether you're looking to be mentored or are excited about mentoring someone else (depends, of course, how far along you are in your profession), professional associations and friendships will help you discover the right person to connect with, and you may learn there are communities where you feel a greater sense of belonging.

- **Access to resources.** An association such as the EO will give you access to conferences, events, publications, websites, and news about the field you work in. You'll become much more aware of the bigger picture when it comes to your industry, and you'll be the better for it.

- **Regain your motivation.** It's easy to burn out when you're working hard to realize great results within your passion. Whether it's at a forum meeting or an out-of-town conference, you are given the opportunity to, as they say, work *on* your business and not *in* your business. That can spark new big picture strategies that light up your professional fire and reinvigorate your passion.

Creating strong life relationships that overlap with your passions allows you to gain more enjoyment in this special Zone of Efficiency. These relationships can also be critical to your professional confidence and progress. I'd like to close this chapter with an example that exemplifies the importance of forming relationships within this particular Zone of Efficiency.

Pulitzer Prize winner Robert Caro is one of the most acclaimed nonfiction writers working today. *The Power Broker*, Caro's mammoth biography of the legendary New York City planner Robert Moses, as well as his ongoing series of books about President Lyndon B. Johnson, have led to him being labeled "America's Biographer-in-Chief."

Yet at the beginning of Caro's book-writing career, he was going broke fast. He had quit his day job as a newspaper reporter because he was planning to finish his first book within a year. That one year turned into five, and during that time, he and his wife had gone through the small advance he had received from his publisher as well as all their savings. Around this time, Caro came home from a day of research at the New York Public Library only to find his wife had sold their home so they could use the proceeds to rent a cheap apartment and buy food to eat while he finished the book.

Caro, like me, had been soldiering on with his passion without the support of any other authors. He just didn't know anybody who was doing what he was doing, nor did he reach out. Like me, he spent five years working nonstop on something he was obsessed with, not really sure if it was going to work out.

As Caro relates in his recent book, *Working*, he was finally able to gain a seat in a special research room at the New York Public Library, reserved for biographers such as himself, to make their work a little easier. He and the other writers could request reference books, and library staff would bring them around on a cart, rather than them having to constantly go and dig them out of the archives. (Obviously, this was before the internet.)

For a while, Caro didn't speak to the other authors in this special room. Everyone was working diligently on their own books, so intruding on their time didn't seem appropriate—plus, since he was still unpublished, he felt intimidated. Most of these men were writers he knew and admired. And frankly, he felt a little ridiculous—he had been working on this one book for years and had little to show for it. He was sure they would laugh at him if he told them of his predicament.

Then one day, he looked up from taking notes and saw James Flexner, the award-winning author of three books about George Washington, staring down at him. Flexner told him he was working on his fourth volume about Washington and asked Caro what he was up to. After Caro told him about his book, Flexner asked him the question Caro had been dreading—how long had he been working on it?

A hesitant Caro finally told him it had been five years. Flexner's reply? "Oh, that's not so long. I've been working on my Washington for nine years." Caro's reaction? As he wrote in his book, "I could have jumped up and kissed him, whiskers and all."

I understood exactly how he felt because in that moment Caro received the same glorious gift I did when I joined the EO chapter in Tampa—validation. He began to talk to the other writers in the room and found out it had taken another author seven years to write his biography of Franklin and Eleanor Roosevelt. Caro was able to calm down about his work as he realized he wasn't crazy—this was just how long it took to research and write this kind of book (a book that went on, by the way, to not only win Caro one of his Pulitzer Prizes but was also named by the Modern Library as one of the hundred greatest books of the twentieth century). He soon was invited to lunches with the other authors and began to learn from their experiences. Caro pushed on with renewed purpose—and it *only* took him two more years to finish the book.

Developing personal relationships with others who love what you love can make a huge difference to your professional outlook and success, if you open yourself up to them. They understand you, you understand them, and you can all help each other, as well as enjoy each other's company.

CHAPTER 7

Zone of Efficiency 3

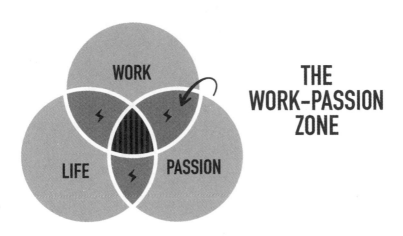

In this particular Zone of Efficiency, the overlap between work and passion has both monetary and nonmonetary effects, which means you may be able to get paid for what you love to do; however, this isn't required for the Zone of Efficiency to have a positive effect on your Zone of Life Satisfaction. Much of what I discuss in this chapter involves getting paid directly for your passion through skill-based fee-for-service opportunities since this is a large interest within the workforce today. But I don't want to minimize the fact that you don't need to get paid directly for your service to grow this Zone of Efficiency between work and passion. The overlap can be more of an intangible enhancement of both areas. In other words, if you work as an accountant and your passion is gardening, you don't have to find a way to get paid to garden; however, you may consider being an accountant for a garden supply store because your passion will most likely make your job a better experience.

Here's another example: if you work as a nurse and your passion is your church/religion, then an overlap enhancement may be to volunteer your time in a free medical clinic sponsored by a religious organization. This will add significant value to your full-time job because you will be satisfied with the volunteering you do on a regular basis. And here's the last example: if you work in sales and your passion is music, you many consider a career in selling musical instruments. But if this kind of position is not available, maybe you can find a job that has a continuing education program that will allow you to use the money you earn to take music lessons.

I discovered this zone when I realized entrepreneurship was the kind of work that kept me engaged and excited. That's the kind of thing that may not do as much for you as it does for me, but odds are you either already have or can easily acquire a valuable skill you enjoy doing. This is something you're good at and that people will compensate you for to use on their behalf. Even if you can't be paid directly for your passion, when there is passion in your life, your work will benefit. This was my experience during the time I stepped back from USA Staffing Services and was working as a physician. Even though I still had passion for patient care, the lack of an outlet for my entrepreneurial passion caused a sense of dissatisfaction with my work.

The Great Recession has given rise to the gig economy where more and more people are hired on a temporary basis or project basis, one job after the other. In today's economic workforce, the gig economy has allowed many part-time passion workers to test the waters of their skills and even get paid for work performed on nights and weekends. The workplace has undergone a radical change in the twenty-first century. For the most part, businesses don't employ people for most of their professional lives as they did in the past—so workers aren't as attached to companies. In a way, we've returned to the preindustrial days, where everyone had to be a specialist. Yes, those specialties have become a bit more sophisticated; they've moved beyond being able to start a fire or skin an animal, but then again, one person's skill may be another's weakness that they are willing pay for.

My point is this—more and more of us are becoming lone rangers, freelance workers who get hired for what we know how to do, as opposed to being corporate paper pushers working toward a retirement watch and a pension. There are new websites popping up regularly to identify people for project-based work assignments. Sure, those pensions were nice and so was that kind of job security, but those days of pension and job security are gone—maybe forever. Now, if you work for a big company, you never know when you might get downsized and put out on the street after ten or fifteen years with your appeal to other employers severely diminished. I also need to mention that I haven't seen a pension plan listed as part of a job description since I started in this industry fourteen years ago!

> **If you develop a particular skill or talent, you are far more likely to be in demand with multiple employers and people who require your specific expertise.**

On the flip side, if you develop a particular skill or talent, you are far more likely to be in demand with *multiple* employers and people who require your specific expertise. You're able to build a client or customer base that hopefully keeps growing and keeps you busy. As stated in a *Harvard Business Review* article, "*It is far more valuable— both economically and psychologically—to be defined by my talent and abilities than to be defined by an organization. Being a 'talented coder' can outlast being a 'Googler.'*"[6] In other words, organizations have become less important, while an individual's work skills have become *more* important.

The result is more and more people are finding themselves thrust into the role of entrepreneur or at a minimum an entrepreneurial mindset even if they want to remain as an employee. After all, when you develop a skill and market yourself around that skill, as so many professionals are doing at the present, then you are in fact running your own business. And that opens up a whole new can of worms when it comes to managing your life. On the plus side, you have much more power over what you do with your working life. However, as Spider-Man's uncle once said (well, actually, it was his writer-creator, Stan Lee), "With great power comes great responsibility."

When your passion is reflected in your work choices, you end up producing at a higher level because you're enthusiastic about what you do—and that extra edge helps you deliver significantly better results. This applies to everyone including full-time parents; when they are able to take time for their passions, they are better parents. The larger the Zone of Efficiency, the better! If you can achieve an increased zone by having a job that impacts both work and passion in a positive way, then try it out! This makes the difference between saying, "I *have* to go to work" and "I *want* to go to work."

Think about the people in your life who have a job *and* have

---

6   Gianpiero Petriglieri, "Is Overwork Killing You?," *Harvard Business Review*, August 31, 2015, https://hbr.org/2015/08/is-overwork-killing-you.

a hobby that pays them. For example, weekend umpires for little league or refs for basketball, educators who tutor students at night, and music enthusiasts who give piano lessons all get to earn a little extra from something they love. And sometimes, they don't even mind if they don't get paid. Parent Teacher Association volunteers, for example, may love to help out at school just because their passion is to enhance the community through volunteering. In fact, volunteering is the ultimate extreme of how work and passion overlap because the selfless acts associated with the working portion of the activity don't earn a dime.

This directly relates back to perfecting your own personal balancing act. When work is just about making money, you're probably going to feel as I did back in 2014—like you're just going through the motions, doing what you have to do to get by without any real jolts of adrenaline to push you forward. You can't help but feel unbalanced; you're doing something you don't particularly want to do for hours at a time.

MY ENTREPRENEURIAL PASSION

Speaking of being a doctor, I am one, and my medical work is important to me. Patient care is certainly one of my passions, but as I mentioned earlier in the book, patient care takes up only a small percentage of my physician duties during a twelve-hour shift. Unfortunately, the vast majority of my time at a hospital shift is spent on writing notes, dealing with hospital politics, and arguing with insurance companies—those arguments can be heated, but that's the only passion I get from those aspects of the job.

My real, stronger passion lies in my work as an entrepreneur for a variety of reasons, but on a related note, I have a strong desire to be directly involved with changing healthcare on a system-wide level through the use of my entrepreneurial skill sets. In fact, my next phase of life will be spent revamping the healthcare system to bring patient care back to the forefront of the hospital business system. (If that isn't foreshadowing, then I don't know what is!)

With that said, as an entrepreneur, I love recognizing problems and looking for creative ways to solve them—which is an ongoing process that any entrepreneur is familiar with. All my businesses sprung out of solving a problem the marketplace wasn't currently addressing. USA Staffing, for example, provided quality operational support for temporary staffing divisions and also provided an extra moneymaking component to existing recruitment companies. Another company I cofounded, Lanefinder, created a technology that filled a need in the recruiting industry for truck driving by matching qualified drivers with open positions. Even my very first business, Handy Matt's, provided a service that most homeowners would rather pay someone else to do than do themselves: painting ceilings.

I also really love being my own boss. There's a real pleasure in watching my business go from a pipe dream to a successful company that employs hundreds of people per year and in watching my corporate employees develop skill sets to enhance their own quality of life. What's also been great is helping others achieve their entrepreneurial goals. For example, the recruitment companies that use our services suddenly don't have to turn away customers who need temporary workers. I can help them up their game and build my own business at the same time.

Finally, it's been great becoming an integral part of the community of entrepreneurs. Obviously, I spend a lot of time on the phone with the owners of these recruitment firms, explaining our services to them. We get to know each other and have a lot of incredible conversations. I learn from them, and they learn from me. Over the last few years, I began to realize that through this process I was networking with anywhere from two to three hundred other entrepreneurs every year—and it was one of the most enjoyable aspects of my work. That's why, as I related earlier, I was so excited to join the Tampa chapter of the EO, a global organization with a membership made up exclusively of entrepreneurs that really opened up many doors in my life.

In short, being an entrepreneur has taken me on an amazing journey. But that's what connecting with your passion does—it takes you down roads you never knew existed. As you travel down those roads, you expand your knowledge base, you network with like-minded individuals, and you're empowered to increase your expertise. All that, in turn, brings you more fulfillment and more life satisfaction.

> **But that's what connecting with your passion does—it takes you down roads you never knew existed.**

First, however, you have to understand what your passion is—and how important it is to your life.

DEFINING YOUR PASSION

I always say a real passion is something you'd be happy doing twenty-four hours a day if you had the opportunity (and a lot of cans of Red Bull) even if you didn't get paid to do it. So it makes perfect sense that I would put a crazy amount of time into my entrepreneurial activities, even though I'm now smart enough to also make room for my family life.

Still, there are many days when I'll be at the office of USA Staffing Services for ten hours or more. That's why when people get to know me, they invariably ask me the same question: "Why do you work so much?" And my answer invariably surprises them—"Well, to be honest, I was only working for two of those ten hours." While this answer is made to surprise, the truth is when passion and work overlap, sometimes the time spent doesn't feel like traditional work even though you are working.

Lest they think I'm just playing video games or taking long naps under my desk à la *Seinfeld*'s George Costanza, I explain that while I may just spend a couple of hours taking care of real work that has to be done for my business, the rest of that office time is devoted to brainstorming new products, finding new solutions to marketplace problems, or even talking with existing or prospective members of our network to learn what works and what doesn't with our current solutions. In my mind, that's not work—that's fun, and typically the time flies by quickly, and I don't feel the strain of long hours.

When I first began explaining my work hours that way, it finally made me realize something important that really informs what I want to say in this book. All those hours I spend at work *not* working (at least in my opinion), they fall into a completely different category than either work or personal time—and that's when I saw that those two categories were so limiting. Passion needs a space of its own. I found mine during those hours at the office that weren't about any work that needs to immediately get done but about brainstorming my way through new business ideas and methods of improving my existing companies.

Before that realization, I attributed the motivation for my entrepreneurial efforts strictly to making money (i.e., working). That's why I started Handy Matt's in high school, and that's why I got into the résumé-writing business in college. Since money had been such a big issue during my childhood, I always assumed I was working like a madman on these businesses just to address that issue. Even when I was pulling all-nighters working on my staffing business while I was also doing my medical residency, I *still* made it about money. My reasoning for my obsessive hours was that if I could get a moneymaking business off the ground, I could put a dent into my student loans. In my mind, that was the beginning and the end of my incentive.

Now, however, I was working the same kinds of hours *when I didn't have to*. USA Staffing was profitable. I was making good money as a doctor. Yes, those massive student loans still hovered over my head, but I was making a good living. For the first time in my adult life, I didn't feel like I was running a race that never ended. I could stop and take a breath, and that allowed me the time to realize an important truth about myself: entrepreneurship was my true passion. And that truth set me free.

How about you? Have you defined your passion?

Here's why it's crucial that you do. When you only strive for a simple work-life balance, it will eventually throw you off kilter if your passion isn't an important part of the equation. That passion needs to be acknowledged and accommodated or you'll be left feeling dissatisfied and unfulfilled because you're not allowing yourself to do the thing you love the most. Yes, if you're lucky, your actual occupation matches up with that passion, but for many (if not most) people, that just doesn't happen naturally. Having your passion match up with how you make your living is a fairly rare occurrence; however, if you define and acknowledge your passion, you can take steps to ensure that you schedule and address it when looking for a new job.

Not acknowledging your passion can also negatively impact

your relationships with friends and family. They can misconstrue how you're using your time and, depending on what your passion entails, make false assumptions that you're either completely wasting valuable hours or working yourself to death. Remember our friend Handyman Joe, the guy who loves to build furniture at night? Frankly, his favorite time is when he's able to engage in that hobby. But friends think he shouldn't keep doing that after a day of doing odd jobs. It's too similar to what he does all day, and it's going to exhaust him. Even his wife thinks he should just relax and watch TV … does this sound familiar to you? Maybe you cave into watching TV because you haven't expressly told your loved ones about your passion.

But Handyman Joe doesn't care about TV. This guy thinks Netflix must be some brand of fishing gear. No, Handyman Joe cares about doing what he's passionate about. But Handyman Joe (like me before I realized how much I loved being an entrepreneur) just doesn't know how to articulate it to the people closest to him. So all they do is make him feel guilty and anxious about his after-hours furniture building. They drain the pleasure from his passion because they push him into second-guessing what's in his heart and soul.

I'm hoping that people like Handyman Joe read this book and understand they're justified in spending that time doing what they love. I'm hoping they are able to fully enjoy that time without guilt or remorse. That, however, can only happen when they *acknowledge* their passion—and help others understand it's something that's vital to their core.

Many of you reading this book may be out there thinking to yourselves, "Well, I guess I don't have a passion. I can't think of one. So … might as well stop reading." Okay, please, don't stop reading because I'm going to talk about how you can uncover a passion you might not even know you have.

Psychology professors Greg Walton and Carol Dweck of Stanford, along with Paul O'Keefe, an assistant professor of psychology at Yale, recently did a study on people's passions and how they get in touch with them. And their findings mirrored my experience of not recognizing my passion when I first encountered it. It's generally not a magical moment, and that sometimes can make you shrug it off. In the words of O'Keefe, "It's this idea that if I'm not completely overwhelmed by emotion ... then it won't be my passion or my interest."[7]

Instead, the scientists discovered that most passions aren't found, they're developed over time. Most of us tend to think core interests are there from birth and that we'll say, "Eureka!" when we're first exposed to them. But this study found that when we don't believe that passions can grow over time, we resist authentic ones because they don't fit in with how we think about ourselves.

As Walton says in the same article, "If passions are things found fully formed, and your job is to look around the world for your passion—it's a crazy thought. It's through a process of investment and development that you develop an abiding passion in a field."

Neuroscience confirms that passions can be developed if we're willing to give them a chance. Before the age of eight, most kids are open to trying almost anything. After that, we get insecure because we want to look good at whatever we're doing. That's when part of our natural curiosity shuts down, which may prevent us from pursuing a passion we're interested in.

---

7   Olga Khazan, "Find Your Passion," *Atlantic*, July 12, 2018.

FIVE STEPS TO FIND YOUR PASSION

I was lucky. I found my passion completely by accident. If you're still on the hunt for yours, here's some advice from Dr. Susan Biali, someone who has made this journey herself (which is why in addition to being a doctor, author, and speaker, she's also a flamenco dancer!).[8] Susan believes there are five steps to finding your passion if you're starting from scratch.

Step 1: Take inventory of your talents. So what are you good at? What seems to be a natural gift you love to use? (Skip those things you're good at and don't enjoy. I have a friend who got all As in math and never wants to solve an equation again in his life!)

Think about things in this category you've done that people have complimented you on. Maybe you dismissed their positive reaction. But maybe there's something there. It could be anything. Maybe you're good at snapping cool photos with your phone, or maybe your cooking has the world beating a path to your dining room.

Whatever it is, give it some serious consideration as a potential passion. Don't worry about if it's practical or if you think it's too different. Different can be good, and practical isn't the point at this stage. This step is all about identifying the talents you have and love to use, even if you think they won't earn you one thin dime.

Step 2: Think about who makes you jealous. This step might confuse you, but feeling annoyed at someone for what seems to be no reason is often a sign that you wish you could be more like them.

I feel as though some of my friends who tried to talk me out of my entrepreneurial ways were much more upset about what I was doing than they should have been. It made me feel as though they were jealous of my being my own boss. I could be wrong, but it was

---

8   Susan Biali, "Five Steps to Finding Your Passion," *Psychology Today*, May 8, 2012.

the type of situation where they might have wanted to follow my path but were too worried to abandon steady employment with a large, dependable company.

So while you are reading this, think about the people in your life. Who do you sometimes feel jealous of? If you can't think of anyone, then ask this question: Who irritates you? Could that irritation be the result of you wanting to be more like them but not allowing yourself to for one reason or another? Be honest about it, and you may be surprised at what you discover about yourself.

Step 3: Remember what you loved as a child. Shivvy Jervis, a Discovery Channel host, producer, and internationally known speaker, is totally living out her childhood dreams. As she told CNN,[9] "Even as an eight-year-old, swinging ponytails et al [*sic*], I would wave around my plastic mic and scrawl little 'scripts' to deliver to a pretend audience. When I was fifteen, I announced with assured clarity to my family that my 'dream job' was to be a producer and TV journalist."

Turned out she was right!

As I noted, after you turn eight, you tend to start limiting yourself and your interests due to a number of factors. Often, getting back in touch with what you loved as a kid can rekindle a passion that you either dismissed or forgot about. This can be the simplest way to discover what really gets you excited about life.

Step 4: When you hate to stop what you're doing, take note. We've all been there. We get so wrapped up in something that we lose all track of time. It can happen to me when I'm caring for patients or brainstorming at my business.

---

9   Jenny Wong and Bryony Jones, "What's the Perfect Job for You? Ask Your Five-Year-Old Self," *CNN*, January 28, 2015, https://www.cnn.com/2015/01/28/europe/perfect-job-career-childhood/index.html.

What makes you forget you're running late? What boosts your enjoyment level to a high you find it hard to come down from? Whatever you love to do, that you feel you never have enough time to do, is a passion—and you probably need to do it a lot more than you are!

Step 5: Make your inner child your companion on your passion pursuit. Remember when I said people are most open to new things when they're kids? Well, that's why I suggest you tune into your inner child when you're on the lookout for your passion. Yes, you want to take your search seriously, but at the same time, you want to unlock that part of yourself that looked on in wonder as you experienced things in the world for the first time.

So when you're trying stuff out, don't be afraid you're going to mess up. There shouldn't be any pressure on the situation. This is a time for exploring and learning, not putting up walls. Trying new things actually increases your dopamine levels in your brain, which brings more contentment to your mood and outlook.

> You can make room for everything if you're willing to make the attempt.

Of course, you must also acknowledge your personal relationships are important, too, and make room for them. That's the life part of the Work-Passion-Life equation. But as I've discovered in my own life, you can make room for everything if you're willing to make the attempt. We will discuss this further in section 3.

When you don't make the attempt … well, read on for a real-life example of what can happen to you.

PUTTING YOUR PASSION IN PLAY

Imagine being so defeated by life you can barely pull yourself out of bed.

That's exactly how Andrew Rea, who was working as a visual effects supervisor in the film industry, felt back in 2015. He was completely overcome by depression and felt like he had no purpose in life. Alarmed by his mental state, he sought professional help—and that help, in turn, motivated him to get back in touch with his passions. He had two of them: filmmaking, where he already had professional experience, and food.

How in the world do those two things go together? Believe it or not, Rea found a way.

With little experience in the online arena, Rea went ahead anyway and started a YouTube channel named "Binging with Babish" in which he went on camera to show viewers how to make dishes featured in popular TV shows and movies such as *Parks and Recreation, Jurassic Park*, and even *SpongeBob SquarePants*. Some of these dishes were delicious. Some were maybe not so delicious (the Ribwich from *The Simpsons*, anyone?). It didn't matter, though, because the YouTube videos were a smash, and soon enough, he had three million subscribers and a new income stream, all from doing what he loved. He felt like starting the YouTube channel saved his life.

The New York Times[10] provided this illuminating quote from Rea: "Even if it hadn't become my career and completely changed my life, the late nights spent tinkering after work would've been worth it. I was cooking again, I was filming again, I was happy again." Rea is confirming what I said earlier in this chapter: the results that spring from doing what you love don't matter. What mattered to him was

---

10   Lizz Schumer, "Why Following Your Passions Is Good for You (and How to Get Started)," *New York Times*, October 10, 2018, https://www.nytimes.com/2018/10/10/smarter-living/follow-your-passion-hobbies-jobs-self-care.html.

getting back in touch with his passions.

In that same article, Laura Vanderkam, a productivity expert, provided more insight into why following your passion is so important. "Life just feels better when you have things in your hours that you want to do. There are moments where time almost has no meaning because we're so happy about what we're doing. The more time you can spend in that zone, the better life feels."

She also offered some very valuable advice on how to make time for getting yourself in that zone, no matter how busy you are. Here are three nuggets of her wisdom:

- Think of time in weeks instead of days. A week is really the "cycle of life as people actually live it," says Vanderkam. After accounting for sleep and a forty-hour work week, you're still left with seventy-two hours to play with.

- Use your time effectively. For example, if you go to bed an hour earlier a few nights a week, you can get up earlier and use that extra time for whatever purpose. It may cut down on your nightly TV time, but it will increase your life satisfaction.

- Turn your passion into an obligation. For example, Handyman Joe could commit to taking a woodworking class. When you pay for something, you're more likely to actually follow through.

Andrew Rea, of course, doesn't need any kind of outside motivation to indulge in his passions. He has millions of subscribers waiting for him to post his next "Binging with Babish" video. However, I want to point out something about Andrew that you may not have realized; his passions actually transformed him into an entrepreneur! His videos have provided him with his own lucrative business, so he has the best of both worlds.

The truth is entrepreneurship allows many, many people to both explore their passions and create moneymaking businesses out of them. Again, the money is not the point of a passion—but how great is it to do what you love and make a living (or at the very least, a side income) from it?

WHY BEING SELFISH PAYS OFF

Irresponsible. Narcissistic. Hopelessly egotistical. These are a few words other people might throw at you—or you might throw at yourself—when you decide to pursue a passion. It's understandable because as I've already said, passion does require a selfish commitment and we're used to viewing that kind of thing in a negative light.

Because of that fact, there are many common damaging misconceptions about the pursuit of passion. In this last section of this chapter, I'd like to share some thoughts about why making room for passion in your life is a big positive and something you shouldn't be judged on.

First of all, *your passion isn't about naked ambition, lust, greed, or any of those other nasty and deadly sins.* Those are about satisfying superficial desires, not about meeting a deep, authentic need such as a genuine passion. Passions usually push you forward through hard work, sacrifice, and effort to reach a life goal you find personally important. You don't pursue a passion for any external rewards but for inner fulfillment.

Secondly, *passion can encompass community and commitment.* Part of my passion for entrepreneurship comes from the satisfaction I gain from giving others employment, adding to the economy, and making a contribution to the area in which I live. Passion gives purpose to your life and often the lives of those around you. Many passions involve building something of value or making a positive impact that has depth and significance. The inspirational fire of passion can create many amazing outcomes.

In the words of one Silicon Valley entrepreneur, "Passion is essential to success, because passion is what leads to perseverance—especially when the dark times come. Anyone can have character when times are good. It's when times get tough that you need passion. Because that's what inspires you to keep going, to persevere. And without perseverance, you can't achieve anything."[11]

Finally, *passion emerges from exploring and engaging with the world, not by detaching from it.* You're not neglecting others just to satisfy selfish desires. Instead, you're motivated to bond with whole new groups of people. You're also happier when you spend time with loved ones because an essential part of yourself is being tended to.

Later on in this book, I'll explore the idea of transforming your passion into an entrepreneurial success, but as we begin the next section, we will explore how to put all three attributes together to maximize your Zone of Life Fulfillment in the center portion of the Work-Passion-Life diagram.

---

11   Joe Robinson, "Does Pursuing Our Passions Really Make Us Happier?," *Huffington Post*, January 25, 2011, https://www.huffpost.com/entry/pursuing-passions-happiness_b_812881.

SECTION 3

The Zone of Life Satisfaction

CHAPTER 8

Keeping Your Equilibrium

Zone of Life Satisfaction: This is a result of having increased balance and overlap between work, life, and passion. This is a visualization that correlates the notion that the more of an overlap, the more balanced you are. This is the result of creating large zones of efficiencies between each aspect of your life and maximizing your life to the fullest.

The Zone of Life Satisfaction is symbolic of how balanced your life is based on the three attributes of work, passion, and life. Imagine you are a waiter carrying a tray with three plates of different sizes full of food. If the plates were spread out on the edge of the tray, it would become very difficult to balance while walking through the restaurant, and a small tilt in the wrong direction could send the plates flying off the tray. However, if the plates were close to the center of the tray, the waiter would have more control over it and would have more control maneuvering through a crowded restaurant. Similarly, the larger the Zone of Life Satisfaction, the more stable your life will feel. It's worth noting that the goal should never be *complete* overlap. This is not possible, as each zone has its own characteristics that require a balance.

Here is the trick as discussed in section 2: the *only* way to grow the size of the Zone of Life Satisfaction is to grow the three Zones of Efficiency because it is in overlapping the individual components that the opportunity to grow the balance of all three occurs. I would like to share a story that highlights this rule.

It all happened at the zoo.

In the summer of 2019, a group of us were at the zoo, and the group included our spouses and our kids. It was a warm day in Tampa, and Laura, Hannah, and I were the first to arrive at the zoo. Shortly after arriving, Krista arrived with her husband and her three kids, and then twenty minutes later, Naim arrived with his wife and two kids. We were checking out the lions and tigers and bears—oh my! It was a great time for all our families, and we enjoyed it to the hilt, but the back story is what is most interesting. Krista, Naim, and I had been meeting on a monthly basis for several months as part of our Entrepreneurs' Organization monthly Forum meeting. Specifically, for me, the EO Forum represents the Zone of Efficiency between life and passion on a personal level, but it also represents at times a Zone of Efficiency between passion and work. Prior to this zoo trip, the three of us had had limited interaction with each other's families, but something magical occurred at this event. The interesting part was that these other families weren't from our personal circle, but we all felt connected in a deeper way because of the various connections we did have. Throughout the time at the zoo, there was talk about work, passion, and life, and everyone involved developed a much stronger feeling of connection. Personally, for me, this trip connected all three areas so well that my Zone of Life Satisfaction grew significantly as a result. I couldn't have planned it better, and even if I had tried, I couldn't have "forced" this interaction unless I was already committed to enhancing my Zone of Efficiency between life and passion by joining the EO. While I didn't imagine initially that the EO would have such a profound impact on my overall life balance, it was sure responsible for ultimately making everyone involved a stronger, more connected group of people.

When I think about balancing work, life, and passion, it's hard to think of a better example than this outing. Here I was, spending time with Laura and Hannah but also getting to know my EO colleagues in a whole new way through a family outing. And at the same time, I was achieving a few work-related goals through conversation and questions.

Of the three circles we all must balance during our busy days, life is often the one that suffers the most. Work? We have to pay attention, obviously, or our income and security suffers. Passion? If we ignore ours, we risk personal dissatisfaction and frustration. That's why our work and passion circles can all too easily dominate our schedule, leaving life seemingly the most expendable. We simply assume the people in our personal lives will always be there for us. However, when we continually blow off those friends and family members, those relationships will deteriorate—and the unpleasant outcome could entail those people choosing to move on without us.

As I hope I've already made clear, it doesn't have to be like that.

You *can* balance your life circle with the work and passion circles by setting clear priorities and creating innovative Zones of Efficiency, as seen with the zoo trip I just discussed. In the rest of this chapter, I'm going to go into specific relationships and discuss some situations that didn't work as planned.

SIX KEYS TO WORK-PASSION-LIFE BALANCE

Since entrepreneurs don't like to be told what to do, I'm going to give you six examples that may allow you to draw some conclusions about potential ways to increase the balance in your zones.

1. **I am not perfect.** I was raised to do my best as long as my best was perfect. If I brought anything less than an A home from school, it was not good enough. Even in high school, even though I was a four-sport athlete, I was still expected to get all As. Whenever my dad coached one of my sports teams, he would encourage me to excel and push myself past what I thought I could do.

    I appreciated the training, but perfection, I've learned, isn't always practical. Sometimes good enough is good enough. The older I get, the more I realize if I don't take my foot off the gas once in a while, I'll burn out my own engine. The healthier option for me is to go for excellence, not for perfection. I still keep my standards up, but I also make room for downtime.

2. **I don't have to take every call.** As I said earlier, technology can make your workday seem like it never ends. Because all of us are now available by phone wherever we go, others take advantage of that fact and bust in on what should be our personal time. People expect us to be constantly accessible—and I used to expect the same from myself.

So sometimes I just need to shut off my damn phone; and remember, the guy telling you this is a reformed phone-aholic. There are still occasions when I'm waiting for an important call and have to take it when it comes in, and that's okay, as long as it isn't a constant. Control the calls, stop the social media, tamp down the texts, and you'll feel more control over your life. And probably less stress too.

> **Control the calls, stop the social media, tamp down the texts, and you'll feel more control over your life. And probably less stress too.**

3. **When I take care of my health, I perform at a higher level.** One of the first things people toss out of their schedules when time is at a premium is exercise (including me … this reminds me that I have to renew my gym membership!). That's why I do it first thing after I wake up—there's nothing else I'm going to have to do that early in the morning, so I don't have to worry about a conflict. I have tried several methods, but the one I think is the best for me comes from *The Miracle Morning*, written by Hal Elrod. In his book, Hal talks about the SAVERS method, which I highly recommend for mental and physical health. Personally speaking, exercise adds to my day. It makes me feel better, more centered, and man, I just love to eat up all those endorphins. And it's not just your body that benefits from exercise, it's also your mind and your entire nervous system. Exercise can put you in a meditative state, especially if you do yoga or a similar discipline that can enhance your mood and your mental acuity.

Your relationship with yourself is as important as your relationships with other people.

4. **I try not to put energy into items that don't move the needle in some aspect of my life.** As part of the Miracle Morning, I write out my weekly goals, and I reflect on them daily. The ability to identify priorities is crucial to managing time. It can be helpful to make a list of what your priorities are, ranked by importance, and then examine your daily routine to see if those priorities are accurately reflected. When things aren't aligned, I need to shake things up and create some new boundaries if needed. For example, every week I spot a new article about morning routines written by successful people—and in every one of those articles, they talk about not checking email when you wake up, so I have implemented this in my morning routine, and honestly, it has worked for me.

Remember, other people aren't in charge of your life. If someone cajoles you into activities that add nothing to your life and take away from what's important, nicely let them know you can't continue to do whatever it is. I try to avoid lengthy conversations with people who just want to chat you up because they're bored, or I consider this part of my work circle if it involves a specific relationship that I am working to improve. Once I was able to trim the fat and eliminate the noise, my productivity, satisfaction, and energy all increased.

5. **I am constantly learning new ways to move forward in all aspects of my life.** Same old, same old. Do you catch yourself saying that to yourself day after day?

I am guilty of getting stuck in ruts because I don't take the time to stop, stick my head up out of my daily routines, take in the big picture, and say to myself, "What can I change to make my life easier and use my time more efficiently?" In his book *The One Thing*, Gary Keller recommends that everyone ask this question daily: What is the one thing that I can do *today* such that by doing it everything else will be easier or unnecessary? It took me reading his book twice to fully understand this concept, and it has dramatically changed my life, allowing me to focus on the most important task, big or small, to accomplish my long-term goals. It could be something as simple as getting your groceries delivered instead of spending an hour going to the store. Or it could be something as complex as changing careers because you don't like what you're doing. I had to leave pulmonary fellowship early because I realized it wasn't my calling, and while that was a very difficult decision in the moment, it was clearly one of the *best* decisions I have ever made. And looking back, it was clear that it needed to be done in order to achieve the success in my life today.

6. **I had to learn that sometimes timing is more important than it seems and large changes typically take large amounts of time.** Did that last point inspire you to make big changes in your life? Great! Just know it will probably take a while before that change is complete. Take it from a guy who spent four years in undergrad, four years in medical school, and four years in residency to become a doctor. Good things take time!

There's a reason most New Year's resolutions fail—people get frustrated when they can't lose fifty pounds in two weeks. Most significant change doesn't happen on your schedule, no matter how hard you try to force it to go faster. Taking consistent and positive baby steps to your goals is much more constructive and a lot less stressful on your system. Over the course of the first ten years of owning USA Staffing Services, I wanted to achieve higher levels of success when it came to gross billings and net profit, but looking back, we were not ready for the amount of growth we are achieving today because the team I have today is superb compared to the team I had five years ago. We didn't have the policies, procedures, experience, dedication, and amazing employees in place in the past, which means we probably would have failed. While we were achieving milestones in growth, we were growing at a rate that allowed us to mature, and today we are stronger for it.

Now that we've explored the many ways work fits into your balancing act, it's time to move on to life itself. I've got a lot to say on this subject because it's the area I've struggled with the most. So stay tuned: the wisdom I've gained from those struggles just might help you avoid some skirmishes of your own.

LETTING YOUR LOVED ONES KEEP YOU OFF BALANCE

To begin with, let's acknowledge that sometimes you *shouldn't* be trying to balance all three circles. Sometimes, a life relationship must be your main priority, especially when it comes to your parents, a significant other, or your children. This is an area where occasionally you don't need or even want a Zone of Efficiency. Instead, put the Venn diagrams aside, and make a point of devoting a significant chunk of your daily routine to those you love most until the chaos settles.

Before I had a wife and kids, it was easy for me to work around the clock without giving it a second thought. After all, my future was at stake, so I gave my full attention to my dual careers in medicine and entrepreneurship. When I began my relationship with my wife, Laura, I made the mistake of not changing up those priorities—in other words, I still worked endless hours. Soon, however, I saw the damage that overtime was doing to us as a couple. Fortunately, I was able to recognize the warning signs from when my first marriage fell apart. And that was a good thing because this time around, I made the choice to evolve and grow as a partner. I changed my mindset, changed my priorities, and with the help of Laura, reprioritized our relationship.

Then came another big shift and another big evolution—we were blessed with our daughter, Hannah. And as any new parent will tell you, life is never the same after your first child is born. I doubled down on my commitment to family time, and as a result, I was able to fully enjoy my relationships with my wife and child. I was able to successfully balance the business with family life after a period of adjustment.

What that taught me was this: as your life evolves, your priorities need to evolve with it. When relationships become serious, you must take them seriously. Otherwise, when you're not making the time to develop those relationships properly, they fall apart—again, I know this from personal experience. You can dig up all the excuses in the world for avoiding the kind of intimacy and respect any real relationship demands, but those excuses aren't much comfort if you end up coming home to an empty house at night.

There are a hundred ways for a marriage to fall apart, but there's only one way to keep it strong and healthy—by dedicating yourself to making it work. You can tell yourself (as I often did) that you're working 24/7 for your family's future, but what you might be missing is the fact that you could be jeopardizing that future through your absence. When you rededicate yourself to your family, you soon discover they appreciate your presence a whole lot more than any extra profits you might gain from constantly burning the midnight oil.

Of course, if you're providing all or a great deal of the income for your family, you can't spend *all* your time with them—that's taking the express lane to bankruptcy. However, one way to create a huge

Zone of Efficiency between life and work is to create a business with your significant other. After all, over 1.4 million couples in America run their own company together,[12] so if the two of you find a viable business model, why not give it a try? Laura and I tried this prior to having our daughter, and in section 4, I will review the benefits and challenges we ran into during this experience.

As I detail elsewhere in the book, Laura and I tried this path, but she discovered she didn't have the same passion for business I did. That doesn't mean your experience will be like ours. After all, there's nearly 1.5 million couples in this country who *have* made it work, and that creates a sweet spot that frequently provides a huge ongoing Zone of Efficiency with all three circles overlapping.

However, be aware that *any* relationship that overlaps with work can be fraught with complications. Let's talk about that next.

THE BUSINESS OF RELATIONSHIPS

It's appropriate to consider your business partner your work spouse, even if you're not married to them. (This applies to business associates, too, someone you might not necessarily be a partner with but a peer or coworker at your level with whom you work closely.) Just as a married couple runs a family together so must business partners run a company. Sure, you don't have to change diapers, but you still might encounter somebody totally acting like a baby

> **Just as a married couple runs a family together so must business partners run a company.**

---

12   James Schultz, "Running a Successful Business with Your Spouse," *Entrepreneur Magazine*, June 30 2017, https://www.entrepreneur.com/article/295890.

(even yourself!), and there's a reason for that: most of us have a lot at stake when it comes to earning a living, so a business relationship can't help but be intense. Conflicts and misunderstandings can easily spin out of control if they're not discussed and addressed, creating a zone of *in*efficiency—where your life relationship with your business associate is threatened by your work relationship.

That's why the personal side of a business relationship is more important than people realize.

When I don't communicate my frustrations to a business associate, it causes as much trouble as when I fail to do it in my marriage. Generally, my attitude is more aggressive than others when it comes to how I like to run a company. I always want to invest more into sales efforts and hiring extra staff, even though it may feel like we're overextending ourselves. "No risk, no reward," is my feeling about that—but that feeling is often not shared by a partner or associate who wants to proceed in a much more conservative fashion. They're wary of spending too much money on areas I might consider to be crucial to growth. This kind of basic conflict can lead to a lot of heated discussions—except, of course, for the times when you stop talking to each other.

And doesn't that sound like a marriage?

The upside? Just like in a strong marriage, differences in a business relationship can provide a necessary balance. If I like to spend too much and a partner doesn't want to spend enough, we're probably going to end up meeting at a midpoint where we're investing just the right amount. The perfect partnership is when individual strengths compensate for each other's weaknesses and different viewpoints are respected and considered. Because you challenge each other, as a result, you both end up growing and becoming better people.

This kind of positive business relationship can't help but create a productive and enjoyable relationship that encompasses all three circles: work, obviously, because you owe it to each other to make the business side operate as efficiently as possible; life because you owe it to each other to respect the relationship and tend to it on its own merits outside of the business; and passion because (hopefully) the work itself is something you both love to do. Achieving the right balance is all-important in this type of overlap. You ignore the business or personal aspects of this kind of relationship at your own peril—and if you're not able to clearly communicate your passions to your associate, they won't understand where you're coming from.

Still, business relationships with a peer, even though they can be complex, are usually much easier to navigate than a friendship with a boss or an employee. The power dynamics tend to get in the way. I've had employees who became good friends, but there were moments when it got difficult. These kinds of friendships can't exist unless both people respect the work boundaries.

For example, just as I wouldn't in the middle of an off-hours, personal conversation start talking to an employee about how they're coming in late every morning, I don't expect that same employee at a company outing to ask me for a raise in the middle of a discussion about our kids.

BUILD RELATIONSHIPS, BOOST BALANCE

While family and work connections are your most important ones, I've found it personally and professionally rewarding to build other relationships in whatever area of life I'm particularly active and involved in. No matter what the venue, whether it's where you work, the neighborhood you live in, or just the coffee shop you hit every day on your way to the office, you'll always feel more welcome and comfortable if you have a network of relationships there that you know will support you. When there are people around who always have your back, it can't help but make you feel more secure and cared about.

In fact, it's an essential human need to have a community in place you can count on. Probably a lot of you are familiar with Maslow's hierarchy of needs, developed by psychologist Abraham Maslow back in 1943. If you're not, it basically puts forth the idea that once you fulfill your most important need at the moment, you seek out the next most important one.

The diagram below illustrates how the hierarchy works. At the bottom, you'll see the basic, most important needs are physiological, meaning more than anything else, you require food and shelter to survive. After you've met those base needs, the next thing you look for is safety, a sense of security in your surroundings. Then we move up to the third most important human need, which according to Maslow is love/belonging. In other words—relationships.

Your first relationship, of course, is with your parents, an easy one to take for granted. Yet it's one of the most influential, if not *the* most influential one. Mothers and fathers provide our templates for adulthood because they serve as our primary examples, and they, consciously and unconsciously, pass on their values and behaviors to us. We can't help but soak all that up as they create countless teaching moments just by how they live their lives. And when they're off balance, you feel it no matter how hard they might try to protect you from their troubles.

As I've said, money was always an issue when I was growing up, and I felt that tension through my entire childhood. Growing up, I saw my dad working for one company and not earning enough to really do everything he wanted to do for his family. That made me want to be in control of my earning potential. And that's an example of how your parental relationships can't help but push your life circle to overlap with your work and passion circles.

I'm sorry to say I took the relationship with my parents for granted a lot when I was younger, to the point where it felt like a chore to call them every week when I was in college and medical school. What I'm learning, now that I've become a father myself, is how I didn't fully appreciate their unconditional love back then and throughout all the years. Luckily, I can now pay them back for all they gave me in little ways. For example, my father loves to go fishing—so when I can make time to accompany him on a fishing trip, I can add to his passion circle and overlap it with the life circle. The bigger the overlap, the more satisfying this kind of relationship can be for both parties.

The same goes with my relationships with my fellow doctors as well, which also create Zones of Efficiency similar to my EO relationships. I work alongside them at the hospital, so, yes, they're coworkers, but we talk about a lot more than medicine. We discuss ways to improve the current state of the medical business as well as more personal matters, such as our relationships with our kids and our spouses and even our financial planning. (Since most of us are carrying medical school debt, this can be a big concern.) Because we share so much about our lives with each other, we're each able to offer a lot of support and help when one of us is dealing with a particular problem.

And we also learn a lot from each other.

Since we're all passionate about providing the best medical care for our patients, we're always on the lookout for the best practices when it comes to being effective and caring doctors. We have monthly conferences where we share the latest medical knowledge and get updates on how best to treat everything from a urinary tract infection to pneumonia. Like my EO relationships, my doctor friends offer a lot of crossover between life, work, and passion—which makes those relationships incredibly valuable and enjoyable.

Most people I talk with complain that they can't figure out how to manage their time so they can achieve balance in their lives. Between work and family responsibilities, they feel constant pressure and always feel as though they're running behind what's left of their schedule. I've found that uncovering these Zones of Efficiency with your relationships allows you to manage your time to address multiple areas of life at once. That overlap can be a lifesaver and, as demonstrated earlier, will ultimately grow the center overlap, resulting in a more fulfilled life.

BALANCE BY TAKING A BREAK

As noted in chapter 4, self-care is important to your ongoing enjoyment of life. If you don't devote time to keeping yourself well, mind and body, you will find yourself losing energy and effectiveness. When you work as hard as most people do these days, it can't help but take a toll. That's why it's essential to take breaks as a way of avoiding burnout.

With the baby boomer generation, those breaks generally came in the form of taking vacations twice a year. Those breaks didn't suffer many interruptions because there weren't any cell phones, so you didn't have to worry about work calls, emails, or texts. You were generally at a vacation destination and away from all the normal, day-to-day pressures of life. You were free to let your mind drift and your body relax. That's one reason why some call those the good old days.

Vacations are simply not as commonplace as they used to be. People often can't afford to take as many vacations as their parents and grandparents could, and our vacations don't last as long. Most people back then worked for companies that paid employees during their time off. With the growth of the gig economy, however, an increasing number of Americans are finding that if they don't work, they lose income, making it difficult to justify the time off economically.

This is an alarming trend, according to a report from the US Travel Association.[13] Consider these revealing statistics:

- American workers had a total of 705 million unused vacation days in 2017.

- Fifty-two percent of all American workers had unused vacation time during that same year.

- Moreover, 212 million vacation days are forfeited annually (the equivalent of $62.2 billion in lost benefits).

Clearly, Americans are giving up a lot of downtime that could be critical to their mental and physical health. It's a different story in most of Europe and Scandinavia, where workers receive four to six weeks of paid vacation per year, typically taken in three- to four-week chunks. Businesses can afford to do this because many

---

13   US Travel Association, "The State of American Vacation 2018," May 8, 2018, https://www.ustravel.org/research/state-american-vacation-2018.

of those governments pay the costs of those vacations due to all the health benefits accrued by those lengthy breaks. These vacations also benefit the businesses, which enjoy higher employee retention rates and job satisfaction levels because those workers are able to take the necessary time to regroup, reboot, and recharge.

In contrast, here in the US, small businesses such as mine must bear all vacation costs. We have to pay people *not* to work, which is a very tough ask—it comes directly out of my profits as a business owner. As a matter of fact, there were many years where vacation pay actually put us in negative territory. After all, we have to not only pay vacationing employees during their time off, we also have to handle the work they would ordinarily be doing, which incurs more expenses if we require temp help to pick up the slack.

However, again, as a doctor, I know the importance of vacations, so we're committed to giving our full-time folks three to five weeks a year based on seniority. We also require them to take at least one full week (five business days in a row) off. Why? Because we want to maximize the beneficial effects of a vacation. Depending on how stressful your job is, it can take three to five days just to relax and let go of that work tension.

There's been a great deal of research on this topic, and it demonstrates the chemicals actually change in your brain when you have that big a block of time off. You feel a higher sense of satisfaction, your cortisol level (cortisol is the "stress" hormone) is reset, and your mental and emotional equilibrium is restored. This explains why when doctors such as me work hospital shifts, we generally work one week on, then take one week off. (In my case, it's three weeks off because I'm back in Tampa working at USA Staffing.) Those hospital work weeks are intense and stressful, usually made up of twelve-hour shifts seven days in a row, so the week off is important to a doctor's ongoing effectiveness. It allows us to be better doctors, just as your taking a week off will refresh you and enable you to come back better than you were before at your job.

I'd like to end this section with one final thought about balancing work, life, and passion: time management becomes less important the more you find Zones of Efficiency and employ them in your daily life. By overlapping your circles as much as possible, you can easily satisfy the requirements of each of the three. You don't have to do the math and split up your time in three different ways—you can serve two to three circles simultaneously if you work it right.

I will be the first to admit that there are always times when you can't help but be unbalanced. You may have to put extra time into a life relationship. You may have to work extra hours because of a looming deadline or an extradifficult task you have to accomplish. Or you may feel compelled to put more time into your passion because a project demands it. Balance isn't always manageable for one reason or another—and that's okay as long as you manage the situation correctly. See chapter 3 to find out how to do so through acknowledgement and communication.

It all comes down to what I believe are the guiding principles for maintaining balance in my life circle. Show respect for your important relationships. Keep the lines of communication as wide open as possible. Don't waste time on relationships that turn out to be toxic or unrewarding. Do try to create connections in any life area where you spend a lot of time.

In the words of writer Chuck Palahniuk, "Find joy in everything you choose to do. Every job, relationship, home ... it's your responsibility to love it, or change it."

Entrepreneurship as a Passion

CHAPTER 9

How Entrepreneurship Can Bring Your Passion to Life

I just came back from Sweden.

To be honest, I never really had a craving to go to Sweden before this phase of my life. I didn't even know that much about Sweden, except it's where both IKEA and its meatball recipe come from. I'm not out to start an international incident here, so let me be clear: I never had anything against Sweden. It just never really figured into my travel plans. But that's all changed—I'm writing these words just after returning from my second trip there. And the only reason I had the opportunity to travel there at all is because of my role as an entrepreneur.

Earlier in this book, I mentioned one of my companies, Lanefinder, which was created to match up trucking companies with qualified drivers. Well, one of the reasons this business came into being was due to my influence in the recruitment industry, based on

USA Staffing Services, and because a technology outfit in Sweden was looking to partner up with somebody in the recruitment space in the US. They had just designed some killer technology and thought it would be best applied to that industry—all they needed was someone to put it into action for them.

That's where I came in. After tracking me down through my company, USA Staffing Services, we talked and decided teaming up made sense for both of us. The result, after many months of hard work, is our new Lanefinder app designed for truck drivers, which we're looking forward to debuting very shortly. Undoubtedly, it will be available by the time you read this, so please feel free to check it out if you're curious about it. (By the way, this is not an advertisement—unless, of course, you happen to be a truck driver.)

When you possess a strong passion and act on it, you'll find many unexpected doors opening for you, as I have. Sweden is just one of the exciting opportunities that has seemed to present itself to me. I'm sure there will be more pleasant surprises like that in the future because the longer my track record as an entrepreneur

> **Everything has its downside, and being an entrepreneur is no exception.**

becomes, the more I'm approached by others for partnerships and start-ups.

What's not to like about that?

Maybe you'd like to find out. Depending on what your particular passion happens to be, entrepreneurship might just be a great way to combine business with pleasure because it's one of the greatest ways to make your passions pay off. And the fact that the rewards continue to multiply for me after all these years reinforces that belief on a regular basis. At the same time, however, I do recognize this way of life is not for everyone. Everything has its downside, and being an entrepreneur is no exception.

In this chapter I'd like to share my perspective on what it means to have the entrepreneurial spirit inside you so you can better understand what running your own business is all about. Of course, this is all *my* perspective, but it's an informed one—after all, I've started multiple companies and worked hard to make them successes. (Spoiler alert: sometimes, they *weren't* successes, especially one in particular I'll get to very shortly.) I've also had numerous in-depth conversations with other entrepreneurs about what we do and how we do it, and I've benefited enormously from their input, which is also reflected in this chapter.

I want to provide this kind of practical insight because I don't want you to view entrepreneurship through rose-colored glasses. The reality of what you must go through to run your own business can be daunting—but then again, it can also be incredibly thrilling and fulfilling if you've got the proper attitude. Me, I went into it knowing almost nothing and learned how to do it on my own through sheer necessity. Prior to that, I had no formal education in entrepreneurship, nor did I have mentors to show me the ropes. That only happened on the medical side of my professional life. I just knew I wanted to do it. So … I did it!

You, however, may *not* know you want to do it. In other words, you may have been gifted with the entrepreneurial spirit but never had the chance to tap into it due to whatever your life circumstances happen to be. Or it just might be you've never even permitted yourself to think in that direction—after all, it's a lot more secure to work for someone else and get that steady paycheck, so it's entirely possible you feel you couldn't afford to take that kind of chance.

And there could be one more possibility as to why you've never given it a go: maybe you don't particularly care one way or another about working for yourself. If this is the case, I would only ask you, Do you have a professional passion or ambition that would be best served through an entrepreneurial effort? If so, you may be so enamored with that specific goal that you find running your own business enormously gratifying—because it will directly serve whatever your passion happens to be.

Regardless of your feelings about entrepreneurship, if you've never gone that route, I'd like to help you understand what it's all about. But let's start with the place where true entrepreneurship takes root and begins to blossom: in your heart.

UNDERSTANDING THE ENTREPRENEURIAL SPIRIT

"The entrepreneurial spirit" is a phrase commonly used to describe the mindset of a person who lives to run their own business, be their own boss, and do their own thing in their own way. Nothing excites them more than to identify a viable business opportunity and run with it. Typically, this is also associated with the people willing to put some skin in the game by using their own savings or assets to get the business up and running.

From the very beginning, many of America's greatest innovators were entrepreneurs determined to shake things up and create progress in their own fashion. You might say Benjamin Franklin was the ultimate entrepreneur—this is a guy who started his own newspaper, discovered electricity, invented the Franklin stove, and even became the first postmaster of the newly born United States of America. I'm still not sure how someone with only one head wore so many hats.

The question I want to ask you is this: Does the entrepreneurial spirit live inside of you?

For example, you might have a nine-to-five job that constantly leaves you dissatisfied. Your time doesn't feel like your own because you're expected to put in all those hours even if you've gotten all your work done for the day. You often have to deal with bureaucratic frustrations and follow rules that can seem arbitrary. Worst of all, you can't help but feel your horizons are extremely limited. Maybe you'll get a small pay raise after a year, maybe you'll get some kind of promotion that's a minor step up the ladder after a few years—but it's hard to deal with the fact that there usually is a low ceiling on what you can expect from your job.

So you might wake up some mornings with the nagging feeling that you should be your own boss. You find yourself gravitating toward other entrepreneurs, taking a hard look at what they do and how they do it. All this might make you wonder how you could put together your own business, even though you may be scared to death of taking that big a leap of faith. After all, if you fail, it's all on you. Then again, if you succeed ... wow, it could be freaking *amazing*.

Inc. (a magazine for small business owners that's done wonders for me) once published what they considered to be the five main characteristics of someone who truly has the entrepreneurial spirit.[14] I think it's worthwhile to list them here and offer my own take on each one.

1. **You're connected to your passion.** An entrepreneur *has to be excited about what they're doing*. I cannot emphasize that point hard enough. Starting your own business is a bit like

---

14   Matt Ehrlichman, "5 Characteristics of Entrepreneurial Spirit," *Inc.*, January 9, 2015, https://www.inc.com/matt-ehrlichman/5-characteristics-of-entrepreneurial-spirit.html.

pushing a boulder up a hill—it's going to be hard to keep it from rolling back down—and when it does roll back, it might roll right over you. But if you stay strong, you'll eventually get that boulder to the top. That requires the kind of willpower that comes from being completely dedicated to the task at hand: willpower that's fueled by passion. I know from experience that when I'm not pumped about a business, it usually doesn't work out because my heart's not in it and that eventually catches up with me.

2. **You always want to know how something can be done better.** When you look at supersuccessful companies such as Uber, Airbnb, and Amazon, you quickly see they have one big thing in common—they completely rewrote the rules of their industry in a smart and innovative way. In the process, they took away a lot of customers from whatever companies had kept on doing business the same way it had been done for decades. Some of the most successful entrepreneurs have planted the seeds of their massive triumphs by simply stopping to take a look at a tried-and-true product or service and asking, How can this be done differently? How can we make the experience better for the customer but still profitable for us? The better the answer, the better the outcome.

3. **You're optimistic about all possibilities.** It's hard to imagine a pessimistic person being an effective entrepreneur. If you feel as though everything is against you, you often end up engaging in self-defeating behavior, such as not attempting to find your way out of difficult situations. Now, being optimistic doesn't mean you shouldn't also be realistic—on the contrary, you've got to have a clear-eyed

view of the marketplace and a viable plan to thrive in it. But it does mean that on those occasions when disaster strikes, you're able to keep calm and carry on, just like the "royal" meme says.

4. **You take calculated risks.** Yes, entrepreneurs have to take risks, sometimes big ones, but they have to make sure they're *calculated* risks, meaning there are good reasons to take a gamble. Making sure you have the odds at least a little stacked in your favor helps you win more often than you lose.

5. **You execute.** Dreamers are important—they often come up with incredible ideas that can change the world. As I wrote earlier, I love to spend hours at the office brainstorming different ideas for not only my current business but other potential start-ups. (I guess I have a little Ben Franklin in me too.) An entrepreneur, however, can't afford to *just* dream—they have to *do*, and do on a daily basis. They have to be able to transform ideas into action or find someone to help them make that happen.

These five qualities are important for an entrepreneur to have. But if it was my list, I would add one more characteristic: I believe you should avoid limiting entrepreneurship to being just about making money. As Ted Turner, one of the great entrepreneurs of the twentieth century, once said, "Money is just how we keep score." The passion for your business has to be there, a passion that fulfills you in some vital way—so vital that if you were to ever turn your back on it, you would be left with a huge void that would be difficult to fill in any other way.

If entrepreneurship does intrigue you, let's dive in a little deeper and see which kind of entrepreneur you might want to be.

WORK-PASSION-LIFE BALANCE

THE THREE KINDS OF ENTREPRENEURS

As a member of the Tampa Chapter of the Entrepreneurs' Organization, I've had the privilege of meeting up with many different kinds of business owners who run many different kinds of companies. At first glance, we all seemed pretty similar: they ran a business, and I ran a business. We were all on the same page. After a while, though, I started to see that was not quite true. I eventually realized there were three very different types of entrepreneurs I routinely encountered—each with very different characteristics.

To give you deeper insight into the entrepreneurial mindset, I'd like to break these three categories down for you in this chapter. One of them may resonate with you and define what your personal approach would be should you want to start your own business.

The Skilled Entrepreneur (a.k.a. the Personal Service Entrepreneur)

Skilled entrepreneurs are people who have a special set of skills and are able to grow a business based on their expertise in that area.

Here's a simple example. Let's say some guy is really great at lawn care—and he has a passion for doing it. In other words, this is a man who likes to get his hands dirty. So he decides to start selling his services to other people in the neighborhood. He gets a few customers to give him a try, he creates good word of mouth, people begin calling him out of the blue to come do their lawns, and suddenly, he has a viable business on his hands (along with that dirt). Now he needs to expand so he can properly serve his growing list of clients. He hires other workers, teaches them to do lawns the way he does them, and after a while, he has ten or so crews working all across the community.

That same process can be replicated by a really great plumber, chef, car detailer, whatever. Any kind of personal service skill set you can provide that's in demand gives you the perfect foundation for your own business. And that business, if you run it correctly, could mushroom into a very profitable venture. But remember the caveat "if you run it correctly" because I'm going to circle back to that.

Most skilled entrepreneurs begin by working for others who pay them to do what they're good at. For example, one of the people in my EO chapter began as a physical therapist who worked for other people. Over time, she saw how her bosses ran things and decided she could do them better—so she went out on her own. I'm happy to say she now runs five physical therapy clinics.

Another entrepreneur based her business on her wine expertise. She started her own wine resale shop and developed it into a restaurant and wine-tasting space. It's become very popular in the Tampa market not only for the quality of wine she carries in her store but also the ancillary activities she markets, such as wine education classes and wine subscriptions. She's proven to be very creative in how she exploits her expertise and provides different kinds of value with it to her customers. That, in turn, increases her ability to make money from her original core business, which is selling wine.

It doesn't always go that smoothly if you're a skilled entrepreneur, however, because you must be willing to make the big transition from expert to business owner. It can no longer just be about how well you do something—it also has to be about how well you master the new and very different tasks that come with running a business. You have to have basic knowledge of accounting practices and how to deal with what will, at least at the start, be an erratic cash flow. You have to know how to manage employees and make sure you can retain the best of them. And you have to market yourself effectively. It's great if you're starting out with an established client base that already loves you, but there comes a point where you must find ways to attract new customers, or your growth will stall. Marketing is the way to make sure your business keeps booming.

The good news is acquiring all the above skills is very doable. I know because I've done it myself. However, I have a mindset that's constantly curious about how best to run a business—I'm drawn to that stuff, and I love to learn all the ins and outs of all of it. Then again, I'm *not* this category of entrepreneur. I didn't originally build a business around a specific specialty of mine. (Stick around, and you'll find out just what kind of entrepreneur I am.)

The primary danger for skilled entrepreneurs is they sometimes focus too much on their existing talents and ignore the actual business end of things. For example, our lawn care guy might get too deep into the weeds (sorry, I couldn't help it) and spend all his time second-guessing his crews and micromanaging their work. Meanwhile, trouble is brewing back in his office—bills are piling up, but no money is coming in because he's not getting invoices sent out in a timely manner. Because he ignores the business part of the equation, he just might end up back with a single-person operation: him, doing the work he loves to.

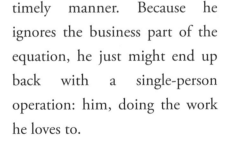

Entrepreneurship is certainly a learnable skill, but you have to want to learn it.

And that's perfectly okay. Some people are better off staying small as a personal service company. Yes, entrepreneurship is certainly a learnable skill, but you have to *want* to learn it. I did when I started my first company, Superior Business Staffing, in college. It was kind of my business "residency" in that it trained me in almost everything

I needed to know in order to evolve it into my current successful company, USA Staffing Services. If you find you don't want to deal with all the usual business hassles, you're better off staying out on your own.

There's one more point I want to make about the skilled entrepreneur, and that's this: the skill they try to build a business around just might be ... business itself.

Let's say there's someone who excels in their management position at a Fortune 500 company. This person routinely wins all kinds of awards and accolades for their business savvy and one day begins to think, "Hey, you know what? With what I know, it would be a breeze to start my own company from scratch. That way, I'd be in control of the whole thing and get all the profits from my hard work, instead of just a paycheck." It's an understandable thought. But what Mr. or Ms. Executive may not realize is running their own business may be a lot trickier than they thought.

Having a high-level position at an existing company is very, very different than starting up and running your own business. Before, you were thriving in an organization that already had all the necessary support systems in place—such as an accounting department, a marketing department, a human resources department, and so on. In other words, when you sat down at your desk every morning, you automatically had a huge amount of resources at your disposal. The entrepreneur? Not so much. The small business owner is often running things on a wing and a prayer. They have to be extremely agile and adapt, often making do with very little. I enjoy that challenge—an executive who's already well compensated and enjoys the support of company resources may not.

My dad, for instance, worked his way up the ranks of his company over many years, and today, he runs its entire North American operations. He's never given a thought to starting his own business; his company gives him what he needs and he likes that security. I'm proud of him for what he's achieved. But to tell the truth, he didn't understand it when I balked at following the same path. And when he watched what I went through when I began my career as an entrepreneur, he thought I had lost my mind. To him, I was just setting myself up for an endless series of headaches. He would always ask me why I wouldn't just stick exclusively to being a doctor. That would provide a steady paycheck to support me.

For me, however, I can't imagine doing it any other way. Different strokes for different folks.

The Opportunistic Entrepreneur

Opportunistic entrepreneurs are people who take advantage of an existing opportunity or product. They're not people who want to start a business from scratch—instead, they look for an existing, proven "sure thing" they can capitalize on so they can minimize their risk.

Many opportunistic entrepreneurs buy into existing franchises. They run their own McDonald's or a Subway sandwich shop because these are known quantities with built-in customer bases and huge brand awareness. All the heavy lifting has been done (and continues to be done) for you by the corporation that started the franchise.

Franchises like these are often called turnkey operations because you're given everything you need to start up the operation; it's just as if you bought a car, sat down in the driver's seat, and turned the ignition key to fire up the engine. The franchisor provides all the systems, protocols, and marketing tools that have worked in other locations—all you have to do is follow the instructions and put them to work. The entrepreneur still has to invest in the territory and ultimately run the business well, but they have a cookbook of recipes to follow that is designed to provide a higher level of success.

I will confess I was briefly an opportunistic entrepreneur. As I discussed briefly earlier in this book, my business partner Mark and I bought a franchise in the in-home care industry from a nationwide company called Synergy Home Care, and Laura was the principal administrator that ran the day-to-day activities. We had a little money to invest, and in return for that investment, we would "own" the Tampa territory. Synergy already had over one hundred other franchisees across the country, so we figured it was worth the gamble. It didn't work out for us in the end, which is why I say I was *briefly* an opportunistic entrepreneur, and I'll explain more about why that was in the next chapter.

What I will say is if you do invest in a franchise, you have to have faith in the systems they have in place—because they will require you to follow them. Your franchise agreement will specify what you can and can't do with the business. To me, that takes a lot of the fun out of the equation, but many entrepreneurs are attracted to franchises for precisely that reason. For them, a lot of the guesswork of entrepreneurship is eliminated (as well as some of the risk) because the franchisor already has a road map laid out for them to follow. The franchisor will also, in most cases, provide some level of training to get you up to speed, so your learning curve on the job is minimal.

Opportunistic entrepreneurs, however, don't have to limit themselves to the franchise route. They can also take advantage of other "premade" opportunities to build a business that generates consistent revenue. For example, you might be inspired by the HGTV channel's renovation shows and buy a home that's heavily discounted because it needs a lot of work. You can then do that work yourself or hire someone else to handle it; it doesn't really matter because the end result is the same—once the house is looking good again, you can flip it and hopefully make a healthy profit on your investment. Subcontracting the reno just cuts into your profits a little.

As a side note, I once knew an opportunistic entrepreneur who "flipped," or more accurately brokered, pianos. Seriously. This guy would find a buyer who was in the market for a baby grand piano and offer to locate one for a price. After the buyer paid him his fee, he then would go hunt down the piano at the lowest possible price (estate sales are good for that), use the fee to buy it, and then have it transported to the buyer's home. He never had to spend a dime of his own money—all he did was take advantage of an opportunity that already existed.

The main takeaway about opportunistic entrepreneurs is that they like to eliminate as much risk from their endeavors as possible. They don't want to reinvent the wheel—they just want to exploit someone *else's* wheel. They're either not creative enough to come up with their own unique business model, or they just want to avoid gambling on something that hasn't been tested. Sure, they still have a passion for running their own business, but they don't want it to be too stressful of an experience. Frequently, they limit their entrepreneurial efforts to being side ventures—that way, it's a hobby, not their primary way of making a living, which further lowers the risk factor. However, they still deserve full recognition as entrepreneurs due to the effort and energy involved in following their passion.

The Problem-Solving Entrepreneur

In contrast, problem-solving entrepreneurs are often the type who take the biggest risks of all because they tend to sail out into uncharted waters. They're the folks who see a better way to provide a product or service—or even create a totally new and original product or service—to solve a problem that in many cases most consumers didn't even know they had.

For instance, did you know you needed a device to play all the music you could ever imagine owning—a device that would fit in the palm of your hand? Probably not, but Steve Jobs did, so he directed his engineers at Apple to create the iPod. Did you know you wanted to be able to watch many of your favorite TV shows and movies through an online streaming service? Probably not back in 2007, but Reed Hastings somehow did, so he pivoted from his wildly popular DVD service and launched the internet version of Netflix.

These are just two examples of visionary problem-solving entrepreneurs who created massive businesses in a space that didn't even exist before. I'm not at all comparing myself to those legendary gentlemen, but this is the category of entrepreneur that I happen to fit in (which you might have already guessed since it's also the last category left to talk about). Most problem-solving entrepreneurs don't create empires on the scale of a Steve Jobs, but my experience is that we still make a big difference to the people we serve.

In our EO chapter, there are several people in the problem-solving space like I am. For example, when the September 11 attacks occurred, the airport security team and the Transportation Security Administration didn't know how to handle the suddenly massive costs of screening travelers at airports, so one of our members worked with the government agency to help them find a solution. Together, they created a marketing company that sold advertising space on the bottom of the containers travelers used to hold their keys, wallets, and other personal items while going through the screening checkpoints. Yes, this opportunity came out of a truly horrifying event in our country's history, but it also solved the TSA's budgetary challenge of paying for all those bins. The advertising fees more than covered those costs.

Another EO member saw that public storage companies were having more and more trouble finding new locations in cities and towns because of zoning restrictions—public storage usually isn't all that pleasant to look at. This member developed storage facilities that aren't eyesores and, instead, are compatible with the community's look. This, of course, isn't an earthshaking concern to most of the people in the world, but to the companies this problem solver helped, it was a big deal. When an entrepreneur provides a targeted solution that works, they have the basis for a successful and decent-sized business.

I've already related several examples of how I started problem-solving companies—from Handy Matt's (people hated to paint their ceilings) to USA Staffing (recruitment firms needed the ability to provide temp workers). My newest venture, Lanefinder, is the same kind of deal.

Here's the problem we found: it's never been harder for trucking companies to find qualified truck drivers, even though those companies are bending over backward to attract them. This driver shortage has been going on for twenty-five years, believe it or not, and it just keeps getting worse. The American Trucking Associations says that currently America's trucking companies are short by sixty thousand drivers on their payrolls, and in a few years, that number could grow beyond one hundred thousand.

Drivers looking for work are just as frustrated. The way the system works now, they put their names in on a one-size-fits-all job board, and before they know it, they suddenly have one hundred different carriers calling them. Some drivers actually end up changing their phone numbers because the calls just don't stop! And the thing is most of the companies calling night and day have no idea if the drivers' qualifications meet their requirements—every carrier is different and has different criteria their drivers must meet. So for the most part, both sides waste an enormous amount of time in communications that are pointless.

Our new app, Lanefinder, is designed to offer a more efficient way of matching truck carriers with the right truck drivers. Drivers enter their qualifications and information into the app, information such as their work history, their tickets, their violations, and so on. Then Lanefinder searches through the available jobs in the drivers' hiring area and only displays the ones they qualify for … problem solved!

Is this app going to result in an amazing business? I think it will because it provides an amazing high tech solution to an enormous trucking industry problem. However, problem-solving entrepreneurs like my business partners and me can never be sure about success with this kind of untested venture—we're literally trying something that's never been done before. That's why problem-solving entrepreneurs end up risking so much when they roll the dice. It's exciting because the upside can be tremendous. It's scary because you can easily fall on your face. And it's fun because you can't wait to see what happens.

Of course, my idea of fun may be very different from yours. That's why in the final chapter of this section of the book, we're going to talk about *you*—and whether you might just have what it takes to explore your passions through entrepreneurship.

CHAPTER 10

Is Entrepreneurship Right for You?

The vast majority of people reading this book probably don't want to become international spies.

Why would they? After all, international spies face risk and danger on a daily basis. They also must outwit and outsmart the competition and make lightning-fast decisions on the spot when faced with a potential situation that could spiral out of control. Often, it feels like there's no time for friends and family because the job is all-consuming.

Well, believe it or not, much of what I described in the above paragraph will apply to your life when you become an entrepreneur. Okay, you don't have to worry about enemy agents poisoning you or putting a couple of bullets in your chest, but you do have to worry about the competition ripping off your ideas or sabotaging you in some other way. You must stay on your toes 24/7 and constantly look for growth opportunities. Often, you have to be able to act on situations as soon as possible to either take advantage of a great opportunity or to avoid a giant setback.

In short, it can be a little nerve wracking—but if you enjoy it as much as I do and your true passion is involved, you'll love the experience and never want it to stop. If all it does, however, is make you reach for the Advil bottle every twelve hours, then this might not be the right path for you, even if your new business serves a strong personal passion. Everyone has different personalities and different preferences. As they say, life would be boring if we were all the same. But since we're not, I wrote this chapter to help you gauge if being an entrepreneur could be your greatest dream—or an unpleasant nightmare you'll want to quickly wake up from.

There are three essential entrepreneurial ingredients I see in myself and others like me. See how many of them resonate with you:

1. You are willing to take a big leap of faith.

2. You are dedicated to being self-sufficient.

3. You have a passion either for being an entrepreneur or for the product or service you intend to provide (best case: you have a passion for *both*).

If you don't have these qualities in place—or the ability to develop them—the going might be very rough for you. Even if you do have all three, it can still be difficult to make the transition to entrepreneur. Why?

The answer can be boiled down to one word: *risk*.

As an entrepreneur, you're going to face it in almost every area of your life. You'll experience ups and downs with your finances, your personal relationships, and even your professional standing. You may have to fail a few times before you succeed—and then take the hard-won lessons from those bad experiences in order to improve the odds of your next venture getting off the ground.

In the meantime, you may start thinking about everything you gave up for this new lifestyle. If you left your regular job to start your own business, you immediately cut yourself off from all the traditional "luxuries" of a full-time job. Health insurance, a 401(k), paid vacations, and sick days … all these perks and more usually go with a solid nine-to-five gig. When it's your own company, however, *you're* the one paying all the bills—so you won't be able to treat yourself as well as an outside company would.

But it's a trade-off, right? I mean, running your own business, that's supposed to be *fun*.

Well, it can be—that's definitely my attitude. But you, you might not like sweating whether a customer is going to pay you (and just how long it might take for them to send that check or make that transfer). Or employees who bad-mouth you on social media or worse, steal from you. Or handling the financial risk of an injury causing a substantial worker's comp premium increase or people suing you over things you didn't (or maybe even did) do. Or the possibility of having to put your house up as collateral to get the line of credit you require to keep your business funded.

Oh, and then there's your credibility and reputation. If your first business fails, it's your name that goes down with it. On the personal front, you find yourself answering the same questions from friends and family members over and over again: "What happened? How did you screw this up?" On the professional front, your standing in your industry could be damaged. For example, if you were trying to disrupt an industry with a new approach and it didn't work out, maybe you won't be taken as seriously in that industry. For example, if I, as a doctor, come up with a new way of treating patients, but it somehow backfires, I'm the guy who's going to suffer professionally.

It could even get in the way of my being hired at another clinic.

Lest you think I'm being overly dramatic here, let me mention just a few of the not-so-wonderful things I've had happen to me at my businesses.

- As I shared earlier in this book, at one point, USA Staffing lost its worker's comp insurance policy, which was one of the foundations of the business. Our premium was paid up, and we had not put in any claims. The insurance company, however, arbitrarily changed their risk profile, and the result was they canceled our policy with only thirty days' notice.

- One of our authorized dealers stole around $100,000 through fraud. That individual is in the midst of being prosecuted for that crime, but that money is gone, baby, gone.

- An important employee quit when they felt they weren't being paid enough. This was at a time when I wasn't paying myself a penny in salary.

- An accountant told me we were profitable (yay!), then after auditing the books, informed me we were losing money (boo!). This is the perfect representation of the entrepreneurial roller coaster, by the way.

- We started our home care firm only to realize we were in competition for workers more than clients, which often meant employees called in or quit for a whole fifty-cents-an-hour difference. This meant that Laura and I were often picking up shifts instead of growing the business.

- We had a state-funded hospital not get the appropriate financing to pay their bills when they had $100,000 in outstanding receivables.

- We spent a significant amount of money on a new technology only to realize the industry wasn't quite ready to use it yet.

- We had a computer programmer work as a temporary employee for three weeks and then file a claim for carpel tunnel syndrome against us. (This typically takes ten-plus years of typing to develop.)

Still reading? Still interested in being an entrepreneur?

If so, I'm impressed. I just threw a big bomb packed with negatives at you. I shined a big bright light on some of the worst things that can happen to your business—and you're still with me. You, my friend, just might have the makings of an entrepreneur.

But, yes, I *was* deliberately trying to scare you (even though everything I told you was true). I wanted you to know being an entrepreneur is not exactly the easiest role in the world to assume. But … it gets better. There was a time in my life when I never would have thought I could survive losing $100,000. That crisis, along with all the others, only strengthened the company and my business skills. For example, that last incident I told you, where the guy sued us for carpal tunnel syndrome? That motivated us to put in place policies and procedures to minimize the chances of that (or any other employee ripping us off) recurring. In other words, the bad stuff made me improve my operation. I hear the same story from every entrepreneur I talk to—whenever they hit a wall, they manage to come out on the other side tougher and wiser.

How do you find the strength to bust through that kind of wall when it pops up in front of you? In the next section, I want to talk about two important resources that can help.

OFFSETTING THE ENTREPRENEURIAL RISK

Based on my own experience as well as that of others, I've found there are two primary resources you can draw on to help you cope with the inherent risks of entrepreneurship. One method is all up to you; the other one is up to everyone else in your life.

The one that's up to you is taking the time to develop a high level of confidence in yourself and your talents if you don't already have it in place. Setbacks can easily eat away at anyone's confidence, but when it's your own business, you can't let that happen. You have to believe in what you're doing and that you really have a better way to do it than everyone else. This is important not only so you can will yourself through any tough patch but also so you can build confidence in your business with the people who are crucial to its success. When it comes to investors, customers, and/or your own employees, the more genuinely enthusiastic you are about your company, the more they'll buy in to your vision and feel good about supporting you. That enthusiasm should have at its base your passion, however it's represented in the business.

> **You have to believe in what you're doing and that you really have a better way to do it than everyone else.**

Confidence is your greatest internal weapon against risk. It gives you the energy to move forward through difficulties and the focus to search for positive outcomes when none are plainly in sight. You will never have all the answers at any given moment—but having the self-assurance to know you can find them along the way keeps your attitude strong and your determination in place. And even when it looks like everything's going to hell, confidence gives you the strength to reach right down into those flames and try to pull it all back to safety.

Now let's talk about the other risk-mitigating resource, the one that might be available to you—or might not.

When most people have a problem in their lives, they lean on the support of close friends and/or family, whoever the most important people in your life happen to be. When you're an entrepreneur, it's also great to be able to confide in your own personal network, even though those people may not exactly know what you're talking about. Frankly, it's nice just to have a sympathetic ear and a supportive word from people you trust and care about—it can provide you with that extra little injection of mental strength that empowers you to carry on.

I will admit I didn't have a lot of that kind of support when I started out. My parents didn't really understand my entrepreneurial efforts, nor did a lot of my friends. They all saw me working endless hours for not much payoff and questioned my sanity on more than a few occasions. I'm thankful I *was* crazy enough to keep going— because I was blessed with a level of confidence that kept me putting one foot in front of the other despite the opinions of others. If your confidence is high enough, it frankly doesn't matter what other people have to say.

That's not to say the support of others has never been important to me. As a matter of fact, it proved to be a turning point in my feeling validated as an entrepreneur. As I noted earlier in this book, when my company made the 2015 Inc. 500, an annual list of the five hundred fastest-growing privately held small companies in the US, my personal support network for the first time actually acknowledged that my business was the real deal and worth the struggle. That's why it was one of the most important awards of my life—because I had finally earned all-out recognition for the company I had built.

LEARNING ON THE JOB

No matter how much you prepare to begin your own business, there are always variables that don't come into play until you're actually in the thick of it. What seems to be foolproof on paper doesn't always work out when you try to transform it into reality. I'd like to share two instances where things did not work out, but I learned valuable lessons about entrepreneurship.

The first instance involved my medical work. As I've related, I wanted to be a doctor from a very early age. And one of the big reasons for that ambition was the fact that in my young eyes, a doctor controlled his own destiny; he *was* his own boss. My practice would enable me to mix my passions for entrepreneurship and medicine and put them both under the same roof. And if that had ended up being possible, I might never have started USA Staffing, Lanefinder, or any of the other companies I've had a hand in.

But a funny thing happened on my way to becoming a doctor: the entire occupation turned upside down.

In 2012 a majority of doctors owned their own private practices. Those numbers began to rapidly dwindle as I went through medical school and my residency to the point where today, it's the exact opposite—only a minority of doctors now have a practice they call their own. The rise of huge hospital-owned chains of clinics, along with the increasing pressures on independent doctors to generate all the paperwork required from insurance companies and the health-care system, meant my private practice dream was no longer very realistic. Or at the very least, it wouldn't have been much fun, given the politics and red tape associated with running your own medical practice.

The lesson I learned from that was this: the economics of industries and the marketplace change all the time. If you start a company selling luxury items and the economy suffers a setback, you might be stuck at the starting gate. Conversely, if you own a string of dollar stores during the same moment in time, you might see profits take a big jump. So don't succumb to tunnel vision when you're running your own business. Take a look at what's going on outside your business door almost as often as you do at what's going on inside it.

Take a look at what's going on outside your business door almost as often as you do at what's going on inside it.

By the way, I still keep my medical business dream alive—in my head anyway. I want to eventually own my own hospital and become the ultimate doctor-entrepreneur. In the process, I'd also love to give back to the community by running a few free clinics. It will be a big plan to pull off, so I know it'll be a few years before I can even think about moving forward with it. However, I've already made it one of my goals by the year 2030 to become a managing partner in a hospital where all physicians who work in the hospital are partners as well; we will all benefit from profitability and strong clinical excellence.

The second instance I want to share is one I've already talked briefly about: the business my wife and I started together, Synergy Home Care. We got the franchise in 2015 and made it all the way to 2017. Along the way, we discovered the following things:

1. We overestimated the demand for these kinds of services in the Tampa area. There were already fifty competitors in the same space, and they had most of the market already nailed down. We also weren't providing a solution that was very different from what those competitors were providing—and

we really couldn't rethink the business because we had to follow the Synergy franchise game plan.

2. Laura found she didn't enjoy running a business like I did. She lacked the passion to push through a lot of the necessary work and considered it drudgery. Bottom line: she considered all the time she spent in the office 100 percent work, not fun in any sense of the word and definitely not a passion for her.

3. I didn't enjoy running the business as much as I usually did due to the constraints of the franchise and the lack of creativity involved to grow the business. I loved trying it out because I was able to do it with Laura and spend more time with her as a result. But the time we put into the franchise wasn't rewarding for her, so it wasn't rewarding for me. We lost money as well as our motivation. Ultimately, it still provided a great Zone of Efficiency since it was time spent with Laura as well as time spent on a passion. But since Laura considered it 100 percent work, it couldn't be a shared passion, so the balance was out of whack.

Lesson number one from this experience is similar to the one I learned from my plans to have my own doctor practice: pay attention to the marketplace. We didn't dig deep enough into the industry we were attempting to enter and paid the price for it.

Lesson number two is just as important: when you start a business with someone else, make sure you're on the same page. Laura couldn't know she didn't enjoy the ins and outs of running a business until she actually did it—but once she figured out this was definitely *not* her passion, we both knew it wouldn't work out long term.

The final takeaway from this experience was I learned I should stick to the category of entrepreneur that I enjoyed. Running a franchise is strictly for opportunistic entrepreneurs, and it made me realize more than ever that I would rather be in the problem-solving camp. I always liked to find new and creative ways of providing a service, but Synergy already had their systems in place. We just had to do the follow-through. That's great for some people but not so great for me.

A FINAL ASSIST

So if after all this, you're still ready to take the plunge and be your own boss, I salute you—and I want to offer you a few more nuggets of advice I've learned over the years that will help you on your way. These are all based on my own experiences in the entrepreneurial world.

- **Associate with other business owners and entrepreneurs.** Entrepreneurship can be very lonely. If you're transitioning from a full-time job, you'll find your old professional relationships won't be of much help in your new role. To me, one of the hardest parts of running my own business was overcoming the loneliness that naturally comes with being your own boss. Your relationships with your employees are very tentative because you simply can't have the same level of camaraderie you'd enjoy with one of your friends. They know you have power over them, and that makes them cautious— it just gets a little weird no matter how nice a boss you are. There's always a wall separating you from them.

The other thing is, at first, there's rarely anyone you know who can give you good advice. Should I reinvest profits or pull them out? Do I dare buy that new expensive car I've wanted for forever, or do I wait to see how we do in the third quarter? Those are the kinds of questions I've always had to answer myself—until I discovered the EO and had the opportunity to finally mix and mingle with others like me. Too bad it took me six years of entrepreneurship before I found them!

- **It's never too late to start.** I've always had entrepreneurial aspirations, but you may not have. But as I've said elsewhere in this book, starting your own business may be the best way to connect with what you're passionate about in life. Ultimately, you may discover being an entrepreneur enables you to have a better quality of life and more control over it—so don't be afraid to try it out, even if it's just a side venture. It's much better to explore a passion than deal with the frustration of never getting to try it out. By making the attempt, you'll feel more fulfilled and, as a result, suffer less stress and inner conflict.

- **If you're highly skilled, you can always bail.** If you made a good living before entrepreneurship, you can make a good living again if you decide it's not for you.

I've known several people who, because they were good at something, thought they could build a business out of their expertise. For a variety of reasons, some of those businesses simply didn't work. Most of the owners weren't making money quickly enough and didn't want to continue to gamble on their futures. So they went back to their previous jobs, and I have to say, their lives seem better for it. They don't mind working for someone else; they find it more relaxing and have more energy and excitement to live their lives. Not only that, but the experience they gained from running their own company often makes them seem more valuable to employers. Plus, they got it out of their systems, like Laura did with Synergy. They tried, they learned something about themselves, and then they went on with their lives. No harm, no foul.

- **Not succeeding is not failing.** Will Smith may appear to be a mega movie star with all the luck in the world, but this is a dude who once made a whole Instagram video about *failure*—invoking John Maxwell's classic advice, "Fail early, fail often, fail forward." If the idea is important to him, it should be important to you. So let's take each of the ideas in that Maxwell quote and break them down.

"Fail early" means it's better to fall on your face when you start a business rather than later on down the line when you're more established and less eager to gamble. At the beginning, it's far easier to try out different strategies to see what works and what doesn't. As for "fail often"? Well, the more things you try, the more setbacks you might experience—but at the same time, the more lessons you'll learn. Those lessons will do you a whole bunch of good the next time around. And finally, "fail forward" is a reminder that you shouldn't let failure define you; instead, you get back up off that face you fell on, you put your newly acquired wisdom to work, and you move on to your next step or even your next business. It beats staying at home and crying into your beer.

Experiencing failure is a necessary step on the way to success. Just write the positives out of it and keep on keepin' on. Even when a business might go belly up, you can still have the time of your life while it lasts.

And if you do, well, you are *definitely* a born entrepreneur!

Serving Your Circles of Life

Just as your car runs more smoothly and requires less energy to go faster and farther when the wheels are in perfect alignment, you perform better when your thoughts, feelings, emotions, goals, and values are in balance.

—*Brian Tracy*

I'm a lucky man. When I figured out how to balance my three circles of life in the Work-Passion-Life model, I also found myself enjoying a more fruitful and satisfying life. I hope the lessons I learned through that process, which I've shared in this book, will help you reach the same happy result.

I firmly believe the rewards I've reaped can be yours, too, because achieving the Work-Passion-Life Balance can't help but bring blessings to your life. Passion brings you excitement, life brings you emotional enrichment, and work brings an income—and hopefully some fulfillment. When all three circles of life combine to create a complete life and the Zones of Efficiency between the circles are maximized, the end result is a large Zone of Life Satisfaction and the greatest opportunity to live a truly balanced life.

> **" Passion brings you excitement, life brings you emotional enrichment, and work brings an income—and hopefully some fulfillment. "**

This brings me back to an important point I want to reiterate: when you find ways to overlap the three circles of work, passion, and life as often as possible, you eliminate a great deal of stress and empower a maximum level of life enjoyment. When each section feeds into the other, you find yourself living an integrated life where each part is acknowledged and no part is neglected. The magic happens through the Zones of Efficiency.

For example, in the last two chapters, I've illustrated how combining your passion circle with your work circle through entrepreneurship can provide a huge and satisfying zone. For most people, work is the least enjoyable part of their lives. Injecting passion into that area can actually transform it into the *most* enjoyable part.

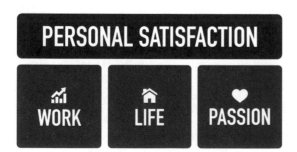

Balance brings satisfaction across all areas of your life.

Let's be real. Life will never be a wonderful and joyous experience every minute of every day. There are always problems to confront and struggles to endure. That's why it's crucial to structure your days so that they're not *just* about those problems and struggles. Make room for passion, make room for relationships, and make room for fun. Most of all, work toward balancing what's important to your loved ones, to your employer (even if it's yourself!), and to *you*.

Serve all three circles of life. That's the secret to ultimate life satisfaction.